How to Figure Out What to Do with Your Life (next) is a comprehensive look at making the big career decisions in your life.

— Eric Boyd, co-founder of StumbleUpon, serial entrepreneur, and angel investor

How to Figure Out What to Do with Your Life (next) is an actionable, step-by-step framework for moving your life and career forward. Jennifer Turliuk's book shines with wisdom from her years of experience and knowledge from the many experts in her network. This is a must-read for anyone looking to level up their career or make a change in their life.

— Ben Parr, author of *Captivology: The Science of Capturing People's Attention* and co-founder of Octane AI

How to Figure Out What to Do with Your Life (next) takes the idea of prototyping and applies it to designing a career that feeds your soul and your bank account. Recommended reading for anyone trying to figure out what to do next in their career.

— April Dunford, CEO, Ambient Strategy, and author of *Obviously Awesome*

Are you feeling lost in your career and life? *How to Figure Out What to Do with Your Life (next)* is an insightful guide that helps set you on the right path in life. The path to success.

— Sean Cooper, bestselling author of *Burn Your Mortgage* and mortgage broker

School does not help you figure out what to do with your life. But lucky for you, *How to Figure Out What to Do with Your Life (next)* does. Read this book, implement its strategies, and share your gifts with the world; you are needed now more than ever.

— Sean Aiken, author of *The One-Week Job Project: 1 Man, 1 Year, 52 Jobs*

Too many people are waiting for someone else to figure out what they should do with their life. Take Jenn's advice of "prototyping" and actually figure out for yourself what you truly are meant to be doing … and in the process how you are meant to help serve the world.

— Yanik Silver, author of *Evolved Enterprise* and creator of the Cosmic Journal

Jennifer provides us with the often-missed bridge from inspiration to action. She shows us how to do what we know we want to do. This book tells you everything you wish you knew at the start, not the end, of your journey through the working world.

— Kunal Gupta, CEO, Polar, and tech entrepreneur

How to Figure Out What to Do with Your Life (next) is an insightful new guide that simplifies and demystifies career planning. Read this book! It will help you make smart decisions to successfully pursue a career you will love.

— Mike Brcic, founder/chief explorer of Wayfinders

Jennifer gives clear strategies to help people find and do what they love, while at the same time helping them build financial well-being for a whole lifetime, not just retirement.

— Kira Leskew, founder and CEO, the Eagle Institute

In this decade of uncertainty, this book is relevant and practical. Many people are asking themselves: What am I meant to do? How do I make the transition? Jennifer has been exploring these questions for many years and shares her insights.

— Cherry Rose Tan, founder and CEO, #REALTALK

Not everyone knows what they want to be when they grow up — not even most grown-ups! In this super smart and accessible book, Jennifer Turliuk breaks down how she figured out what she wants to do with her life — and how you can pinpoint your purpose, too.

— Sofi Papamarko, writer and entrepreneur

HOW TO

Figure Out What to Do with Your Life (next)

HOW TO
Figure Out What to Do with Your Life (next)

JENNIFER TURLIUK

DUNDURN
TORONTO

Publisher and acquiring editor: Scott Fraser | Editor: Michael Carroll
Cover and interior designer: Laura Boyle
Printer: Marquis Book Printing Inc.

Library and Archives Canada Cataloguing in Publication

Title: How to figure out what to do with your life (next) / Jennifer Turliuk.
Other titles: Figure out what to do with your life
Names: Turliuk, Jennifer, author.
Description: Includes bibliographical references and index.
Identifiers: Canadiana (print) 20200343254 | Canadiana (ebook) 20200343270 | ISBN 9781459747494 (softcover) | ISBN 9781459747500 (PDF) | ISBN 9781459747517 (EPUB)
Subjects: LCSH: Vocational guidance. | LCSH: Vocational interests. | LCSH: Career changes.
Classification: LCC HF5381 .T87 2021 | DDC 331.702—dc23

We acknowledge the support of the Canada Council for the Arts and the Ontario Arts Council for our publishing program. We also acknowledge the financial support of the Government of Ontario, through the Ontario Book Publishing Tax Credit and Ontario Creates, and the Government of Canada.

Printed and bound in Canada.

VISIT US AT

 dundurn.com | @dundurnpress | dundurnpress | dundurnpress

Dundurn Press
1382 Queen Street East
Toronto, Ontario, Canada
M4L 1C9

To my family

Contents

Introduction

> He has achieved success who has lived well, laughed often, and loved much; who has gained the respect of intelligent men and the love of little children; who has filled his niche and accomplished his task; who has left the world better than he found it, whether by an improved poppy, a perfect poem, or a rescued soul; who has never lacked appreciation of earth's beauty or failed to express it; who has always looked for the best in others and given the best he had; whose life was an inspiration; whose memory a benediction.
>
> — BESSIE ANDERSON STANLEY

If you're stuck in a job you hate, you're unfortunately not alone. In fact, astonishingly, more than 80 percent of Americans and 75 percent of Canadians are dissatisfied with their jobs.[1]

I was unhappy with the career path I entered just after graduation from university. I woke up late, went to sleep when I got home at 6:00 p.m., and developed all sorts of aches and pains I had never felt before. It took me a while, but I finally gathered the courage to quit. Like many people, I'd put more thought and effort into getting the job than into figuring out if it was something I actually wanted. There's plenty of research and advice out there on how to write the perfect résumé and ace that interview. But when it comes to figuring out what you want to do with your life, the strategies aren't so clear.

I realized that although I could predict and pontificate about a career path that might make me happier, I'd never actually know until I was in the thick of it. I had an idea that I might like to do something related to entrepreneurship but didn't exactly know what that meant. Did I want to join a startup? Start my own? Try to get into venture capital? Join or start a non-profit? Do international development work abroad?

More importantly, I didn't know how I could figure it out without a huge investment of time, like starting another full-time job with a new company.

But then I had a different idea. I decided to enter a competition to shadow Dave McClure, who founded the accelerator 500 Startups. Being selected as one of the top six finalists gave me the kick I needed to quit my job, fly down to Silicon Valley, and begin what I call a "self-education program" on something they don't teach you in school but is arguably the most important thing of all: what I wanted to do with my life.

What is that? I run my own company and make a competitive salary. I control my days and who I spend time with. My company makes a difference in the lives of our customers, staff, and community members — and has strong potential to grow. Sometimes I have bad days, but many are good. Certainly, there are many more good days than I used to have. And the work is fulfilling. I learn new things every day, and I've met the most amazing people through my involvement with this business. I can't think of anywhere I'd rather be. In this book, I share the Career Design Process I created to get to this point, made up of ideas from the quantified self movement (users and makers of self-tracking technological tools), design thinking, lean startup methodologies, and more.

So what did I do during my self-education program? So many things — and I'll tell you all about them in this book. Over the course of a few months, I began cold emailing anyone I could think of who I was interested in meeting and learning from. To my surprise, I had a shockingly high response rate. I met with the founders of Airbnb, Square, Kiva, Mint, Color, and many more, and also with various investors and professors in the Bay Area. I asked them about their career paths, how they'd come to be where they were now, and what recommendations they had for figuring out my next move.

And I didn't stop there. I also volunteered at major conferences such as DEMO and Founder Showcase so I could meet more people and attend the talks for free. I checked out various events and lectures in the region, and even sat in on classes at Stanford University, which the professors were kind enough to let me attend. Finally, to get a full holistic experience, I lived in a co-op in Palo Alto, California, and had an amazing time learning about cooking, co-operative living, and various lifestyles.

One of the most important conversations I had was with John Krumboltz, an international career expert who teaches career coaching at Stanford. He advocated an idea that stuck with me: testing out the different career experiences I was interested in, in the most low-commitment way I could for each option. I had just been introduced to the entrepreneurial concept of "minimum viable product" — an interesting parallel, I thought — so I decided to apply these same principles to deciding what to do next with my career.

I began "prototyping" the different work experiences I was considering — dipping my toe in each, so I could figure out which I liked best. Again, using my favourite tactic of cold emailing, I reached out to and secured "shadow experiences" with companies, including Launchrock (a 500 Startups company), Dojo, Causes (started by Sean Parker), Kiva, the Stanford d.school, and Ashoka (a non-profit that supports entrepreneurship). I spent one to five days with each company, not only learning from them but also assisting them wherever I could. At Causes, I helped produce success reports for clients and sat in on strategy meetings and interviews with potential hires. At Kiva, the then CEO Matt Flannery let me follow him around for the day (the literal definition of a shadow) and experience "a day in the life," complete with accompanying him on his daily walk in the park to clear his head.

So what did I learn through all of this? I realized that I wanted to pursue my own business as soon as possible. In one of the classes I sat in on at Stanford, the professor asked the students how they wanted the world to be different when they died. I knew then that not only did I want to be passionate about what I was doing — I wanted others to be, too. I wanted my business to do something that helped other people find and pursue career activities they were passionate about, and I've worked toward that objective ever since.

But looking back, I'm so happy I took the time to prototype my different career options and am grateful for the fact that it was nearly free to do so — much cheaper than an M.B.A., which many people say they take to figure out what to do with their lives. I learned more in those few months than I had in years.

And whether or not you can spare a few months off work, you can learn like that, too. If you're not quite sure about your career path, you can pick a few things you think you'd rather be doing and then prototype them yourself by setting up experiences in which you can try out your different options. Find companies you'd like to work for and individuals whose career paths you admire and then reach out to them to see if you can shadow them for an afternoon, a day, or a week. This book will show you how. Try informational interviews, volunteering, internships, and more. And don't be surprised when they say yes, or even if many of these experiences lead to job offers — without you even asking for them.

One thing that really surprised me during my experience was how easily approachable, open, and helpful most people are. Cold emailing has become perfectly normal, as has saying, "I saw you on Twitter and thought you seemed interesting, so I wanted to reach out." This is the first time in history that people's career interests and hobbies are listed online and are easily searchable — and it's an amazing opportunity to create your own network beyond just the people you meet in person.

Take it from me: if you're trying to decide on your next step, it's an opportunity you can — and should — take advantage of.

Now, am I an expert on success? It depends on how you look at it. I'm definitely still in the process of figuring everything out, since I believe everyone is for the entirety of their lives, but so far some people have said I've managed to figure out, sort through, and accomplish some pretty amazing things for my age. I was inspired to write this book because of the reaction I got from an article I wrote for *Forbes* about my Career Design Process.[2]

When I set out to write the piece for a blog called *The Daily Muse*, my main aim was to get it on *Forbes*, one of *The Daily Muse*'s distribution partners. I didn't expect it to go anywhere or to get much traffic — I just wanted to have an article on *Forbes*, and that was that. I thought it would be pretty cool. *The Daily Muse* said it would definitely be able to put the article on its site and would try its best to get the piece on *Forbes* but couldn't promise anything.

So the article went up on *The Daily Muse*'s website, and the next day, imagine my surprise when I got an email from a reader saying, "Hey, I loved your article on *Forbes*." I replied, "What article on *Forbes*? Can you send me the link?" And the emails didn't stop from then on. In fact, years later, they still haven't ceased, which has provided me with one of the most remarkable experiences of my life. Either every week or a couple of times a month, I hear from incredible people trying to navigate their next steps in life. Some of them are extremely accomplished — and it's a real comfort to know that even *they* don't have everything figured out. Everyone's just trying to make the best of what they've been given in this world. When you walk down the street, everyone you see along the way is attempting to make life as good as possible for themselves, their families, and in general, the people around them. It's amazing!

I think the reason the *Forbes* article got so much traction was because it was something of a unique story. Within a short period of time, the piece had over 250,000 views, was reprinted in New York City's daily morning newspapers, was featured on *LinkedIn Today* and the *Forbes* "Most-Read and Top Trending Stories" lists for more than a week, and resulted in multiple requests for book proposals. Now it's up to over 1.5 million views. And it's also led to thousands of emails, tweets, LinkedIn and Skype requests, and even some phone calls.

At first the experience was a bit overwhelming. And to some extent, it still is. But I feel exceptionally privileged to help so many people figure out what to do with their careers, figure out how they can make the biggest impact for themselves and for the world, and figure out how they can be happier than they were when they first got in touch with me.

I've been doing career coaching for a number of years. It's one of my favourite things to do because I'm a strong believer in the power of human potential, especially when it's aligned with the strengths and desires of the individual and the world. I also believe that what you do in your career has a huge impact on the rest of your life — either positive or negative. So it's important to make sure it's positive! The halo effect of your work can affect everything from your family life, friends, physical shape, and spending, to sicknesses, bodily problems, and many other things.

What topics will we cover? We'll start with a bit of background about me and my career choices so you can get an idea how I came to develop my methodologies. Then I'll show you how to develop your own ideas of what you might like to do as your next career move, based on what you like, what you're good at, what the world needs, what you can make money from doing, and a series of experiments I'll guide you through to set yourself up. We'll also cover self-education programs and the ability to train yourself to be virtually anything you want to be. Once we've begun figuring out what you want your next career move to be, we'll shift to definitive strategies for getting what you want, dealing with everything from cover letters and résumés to job search tools, online presence, networking, interviewing, and the day-to-day of being in your new position. This book is both for people who want to find a job and for those who want to be entrepreneurs. It will help you figure out what you want to do and then go get it. If you're unemployed and looking for a job, this book will help you with that, too.

My writing is based on more than 10 years of career counselling, personal career experience, interviews with countless successful people about how they got to where they are today, hundreds of books I've read about career choices (plus many more articles), and the education I've received in business, marketing, psychology, happiness, and storytelling. I've helped my clients land jobs at Google, Procter & Gamble, Kelson, and many others; make investments; sell franchises; and get into prestigious incubators.

Everyone wants to be happy with what they're doing in the world and how they're spending their time. I've interviewed some amazing people about how they created careers they love — and how you can do that too. Some of the people I spoke with and/or interviewed in preparation for writing this book include Peter Thiel (co-founder and former CEO of PayPal), Dave McClure* (angel investor who founded the 500 Startups incubator), and the founders and CEOs of Airbnb (Joe Gebbia), Square (Randy Reddig), and Kiva (Matt Flannery). I also leverage my experience participating in Singularity University's Graduate Studies Program at the National Aeronautics and Space Administration (NASA) to discuss not just where the market stands today in terms of work and job opportunities but what the future of work will look like — as told to us by Sophie Vandebroek, the chief technology officer of Xerox, and many others — and how you can fit into it.

I've written this book with the hope that I inspire others to follow their passions in a way that makes a positive difference in the world. If I do that, I'll have truly succeeded.

Now, let's begin.

---

* Dave McClure has since resigned from 500 Startups.

The Career Crisis

Only those who will risk going too far can possibly find out how far one can go.

— T.S. ELIOT

Are you having a hard time figuring out to do with your career? Are you dissatisfied with your job? You're not alone. Nowadays, people feel worse about their jobs and work environments than ever before[1] — over 80 percent of Americans and 75 percent of Canadians are unhappy with their jobs[2] — and the statistics are similar around the world. In 2011, a shocking 32 percent of workers said that they wanted to leave their jobs and 25 percent had no definite plans to leave but were apathetic and even more negative about their work than employees considering an exit.[3] Employee turnover is at an all-time high, and there's no sign that any of these statistics will improve. And at the time this book was in production, the COVID-19 pandemic dramatically affected both the work environment and unemployment.

Why is this important? Well, people who feel successful in their work lives are twice as likely to feel very happy than those who don't, regardless of income level.[4] The opposite of this is "learned helplessness," where people simply give up and stop trying to succeed, and we're beginning to see more and more of this with the number of workers worried about being laid off at an all-time high of 30 percent.[5] Low job satisfaction is correlated with high rates of anxiety, depression, psychosomatic symptoms, heart disease, and poor mental health[6] — all of which can also lead to problems with family and romance. Job dissatisfaction is terrible for the world.

Most of my classmates from university who I've talked to since graduation are unhappy about or only okay with their jobs, and there are consequences when you don't do something you like. Most people only think about the financial aspects of taking a risk to do what they love. But what about the risks of doing something you dislike: such as doing something that goes against your values, doesn't let you reach your full potential, or involves working with people you dislike? For me, this meant I got depressed, had health issues (back and wrist pains and a random eye twitch for the first time in my life), and wasn't performing. It was one of the worst times of my life. I think this quote from the book *The Monk and the Riddle* perfectly exemplifies how there are more risks to consider than just financial ones:

> Personal risks include the risk of working with people you don't respect; the risk of working at a company whose values are inconsistent with your own; the risk of doing something you don't care about; and the risk of doing something that fails to express — or even contradicts — who you are. And then there is the most dangerous risk of all: the risk of spending your life not doing what you want on the bet that you can buy yourself the freedom to do it later.[7]

Along those lines, there have been plenty of examples of people working in jobs they hate to save up for retirement and then promptly dropping dead very shortly after retiring.

For corporations, low job satisfaction leads to lower productivity and innovation, as well as increased recruiting costs due to high turnover. America's disengagement crisis costs corporations a staggering $300 billion in lost productivity annually.[8] The simple fact is, workers perform better when they're happily engaged in what they do. Even worse, job dissatisfaction also leads to lower levels of innovation. If you compare the job satisfaction and innovation rates over time, you start to see some patterns.

With an army of unhappy workers, how can we expect to solve the grand global challenges? How can we make a major impact on issues such as climate change or poverty if we aren't able to bring our full energy to work?

Job Satisfaction

Only 45 percent of American workers were satisfied with their jobs in 2009, down from 61 percent in 1987.

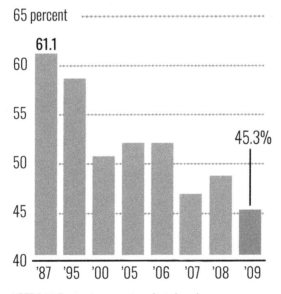

NOTE: Initially reports were not conducted yearly.

FIG. 1: *Comparison of job satisfaction rates from 1987 to 2009 in the United States.*
Source: Copyright © 2021 The Conference Board, Inc. Content reproduced with permission.

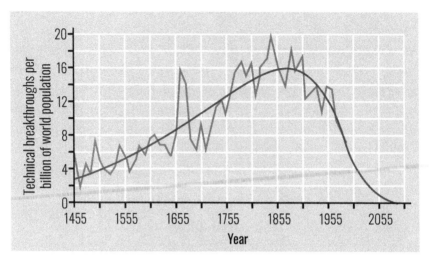

FIG. 2: *Global technological innovation rates from 1455 to 2055.*
Source: Jonathan Huebner, "A Possible Declining Trend for Worldwide Innovation," Technological
Forecasting and Social Change *72, no. 8 (October 1, 2005): 980–86. Copyright © 2021 Elsevier.*

I became passionate about this issue when working in my first job out
of university — a marketing position at a large corporation. Many of my
classmates viewed landing this role as a huge success, and I also thought
I'd be happy in it. However, I became extremely dissatisfied almost as
soon as I began working there, which had a huge effect on my whole life.
I became extremely depressed, and every night I'd get home from work
and fall asleep around 6:00 p.m. because I didn't have enough energy to
do much of anything else.

Yet it was extremely difficult for me to muster the courage and ability to actually leave the job. I looked around and saw that in such a bad
economy many people were having a hard time even *finding* a job — so
who was I to complain? Because I didn't like what I was doing, I started
to feel as if I was underperforming, which made me begin to lose confidence in myself. Maybe I couldn't get a better job. And even if I could,
I thought surely the "black hole" that would result on my résumé from
leaving a job within less than a year would blacklist me from ever getting
further positions or having a good career. Most of all, I had no idea what
to do next. Sound familiar?

I realized that there weren't many good tools available to help me choose what type of job I'd be happier in — I'd done extensive career testing that had said the corporate job was a good choice. I wasn't sure what I was passionate about and whether I wanted to work for a non-profit or for-profit, or start my own company. So I quit my job and set up my own self-education program where I shadowed at six different companies for one to five days each, learning from them but also helping them wherever I could. It made me realize I wanted to start a for-profit startup that helps people find and choose careers they're passionate about. This concept of validating what you actually like is a major topic of this book.

Since my self-education program, I've done many things that I wouldn't have been able to do if I'd stayed at a job where I was so unhappy. I launched an accelerator program for young entrepreneurs in Toronto, where many participants ended up leaving their jobs, receiving multiple investment offers, and opening franchises of their businesses. I organized programming classes for students in Chile on programming languages such as Python that they don't normally teach there. Then I went to Singularity University to try to figure out how to flip the statistics so that 80 percent of people are satisfied with their jobs ... or 100 percent.

How can we solve this pressing issue? For individuals, the single most important factor to employee engagement is simply to feel you're making progress in meaningful work, which can lead to joy and excitement and improve performance — a positive upward spiral. This alone carries people through many things, including long hours and low pay. It doesn't mean picking a job off a list of the 10 happiest occupations or choosing any noble cause and devoting your life to it — it entails figuring out what kind of work is truly meaningful to you as an individual and then finding a job that allows you to do it, even if it has a low salary, although that doesn't always have to be the case! The difference between the happiest and the most hated jobs is whether the job feels worthwhile or pointless. There are a number of different techniques to figure this out.

To provide meaningful work, companies need to redesign their human-resources strategies. Some, like Google and Facebook, are doing a great job providing supportive and flexible work environments. Others are asking talented people to "design their dream jobs" and then creating roles around them instead of trying to fit them into one-size-fits-all job descriptions. As such, individuals need to find companies and jobs that align with their passions and skills. Currently, most recruiting focuses on skills and not passions, but as I've mentioned, passion is one of the most important factors toward doing good work.

Corporations need to ensure they offer an environment that's supportive for employees. They should train managers on the importance of supporting progress, removing barriers, and giving workers a direct line of sight to customers and the impact of what they do so they can see meaning in their work. Other ways to increase engagement are to allow work to be done in self-organizing teams and to provide options for career-advancing work, flexible schedules, and telecommuting. Governments can improve mobility and opportunity through education reform, pro-growth policies, and an entrepreneur-friendly economy. Companies that don't delight customers don't survive, but I would also argue that companies that don't delight their employees won't survive, either. Working adults spend more of their waking hours at work than anywhere else, so let's make sure those hours are life enhancing.

With more people in developed countries finding careers they're passionate about, there will be more happiness, less health issues, and more good work on critical issues such as the environment and poverty in the developing world. So, my ask of you is to make sure you find and do work you're extremely passionate about and help others do the same. Our planet needs it.

WHAT NOT TO DO

First, let's start with what *not* to do:

1. **Don't just blindly do what your parents tell you to do:** Seriously, don't. Now I love my parents very much, but let's face it, parents have a different objective for your career than you do — security. Your parents want you to be safe and have enough money to live off of, so obviously most will, either consciously or unconsciously,

point you in the direction of the most well-paying, secure option. Do you *really* think they're going to be excited about the fact that you want to jaunt off to Africa to take a barely paying job helping local entrepreneurs? No! But that sounds pretty badass to me! I can't even believe the number of people I know who, when I ask them why they picked the job or career they're doing, answer that it's because their parents told them to. For the love of God, don't become one of those people. If your parents really love you, they'll get over it and support you in whatever you do. I know mine did. At an early point in your life, pay doesn't matter as much as great experience that can set you up for future possibilities of high pay. Richard Branson and Oprah Winfrey, for example, both made very little in the early days of their careers. So unless you have massive amounts of debt, or a significant other and kids you're supporting, choose a great experience over high pay, because it's better to enjoy every day than to hate work and end up blowing the extra cash, anyway, on partying and vacations to try to make things palatable. You can always get more money, but you can't always get more time.

2. **Don't believe the hype that you need experience before doing what you love:** This is simply not true. Don't get convinced that marketing dish detergent or pushing boxes around on slides will help you be a successful entrepreneur, fashion designer, or whatever your dream is. Know that some of the most successful founders (e.g. of Google, Apple, et cetera) had little or no corporate experience at all. As a *Harvard Business Review* article put it, "To paraphrase Warren Buffett, a career strategy based on doing what you *dislike today* so that you can do what you *like tomorrow* is as wise as deferring *sex* while young so that it can be enjoyed in old age."[9] Happiness is wanting what you have — so aim for that instead of having a deferred life enjoyment plan.

3. **Don't listen to anyone except yourself:** At the end of the day, all that really matters in your career decisions is you and what you want, and ideally, what positive impact you want to have on the world. Everyone looks at things through different lenses based on their experiences, so no one can have the right answer for

you — except you! Try to stay away from the gossip about who got what interview, what offer, et cetera. Knowing that information isn't going to help you at all — it will only clutter your mind with useless thoughts that will distract you from your pursuit of awesomeness. Also, mentors and role models are great, but again, don't take their word as gospel. They might have tried something and failed, or not been brave enough to try anything at all. But since it was their life paths and choices, in most cases they'll defend themselves and perhaps advise you along the same path. Remember, you're different — in a good way!

So how are you going to figure out what to do? Keep in mind a couple of points:

1. Career counsellors can't give you *the* answer of what to do. They're good at résumés and cover letters, but helping you figure out what you want to do is way tougher because there aren't proven techniques (career testing is flawed because it only lists a limited number of occupations). Also, to make a good decision you need to decide for yourself, not let someone else do it for you.

2. Other people can't give you the answer of what to do. As I've said, everyone looks at things through different lenses (e.g. failure, success) based on past experiences, so they'll advise you on what they'd do in your situation, but not necessarily what's best for you. So take other people's advice with a grain of salt — even mine. Especially because asking people older than you means they grew up in a completely different time/culture, where, for example, manufacturing was hot and the internet or apps hadn't been invented yet.

3. Remember that most people aren't happy with their jobs. So it's hard for someone who hasn't found a job that makes them happy to advise you on how to find one that *will* make you happy.

4. Also, keep in mind that corporate experience doesn't necessarily help to become an entrepreneur. I met a young entrepreneur who began his startup at age 19 and has been super successful. And it's pretty easy to get sucked in and end up staying in a corporation

for way longer than you wanted or expected to when you began, because they're masters at dangling carrots in front of your eyes (e.g. raises, cars, et cetera) just when your eyes are starting to wander or glaze over.

WHAT YOU SHOULD DO

Now let's turn to what you *should* do.

1. **Devote time to a new career:** This book is for you if you're ready to devote time to a career change. I sometimes hear people say something along the lines of "I want to do more job applications, but I just can't seem to find the time." This seems ludicrously counter-intuitive to me. Shouldn't finding a job that you love be one of the single most important things you do during your life? Forget an assignment that makes up 3 percent of your total work time — this is a matter of where and how you'll be spending a significant amount of your time in your life. Better find something you're happy doing — and find it soon! The only resource you can't get more of is, you guessed it, time.
2. **Do it now:** The sooner you know what kind of job you want, the more streamlined your job search will be. You'll spend less time waffling about and preparing for interviews for jobs you might later decide you don't want. Without these added hassles, you have the potential to find a job you really want more quickly. You can always change later. Figuring out early what potential options you like will allow you to do internships or short jobs in those areas and determine if you really could see yourself working in that area for years on end.

WARNING

Finding a good career fit for you isn't for the faint of heart. That might sound crazy — after all, aren't we all entitled to a good career fit? But the possibility of us all achieving it couldn't be farther from the truth. Attaining a great career fit is like hunting for a needle in a haystack. There's a possibility the day will never come. And, in fact, chances are you'll never feel that one day the heavens have opened up and this is "it" — the dream career you'll want and cherish forever.

At the time of writing this book, I'm not married, but from what I've been told about finding a husband or wife, it isn't really a fairy tale where all of a sudden Prince or Princess Charming comes riding along out of the sunset and dips you into an amazing dance move and the two of you caress and are married days later. Maybe for some people it's like that. I don't mean to sound cynical, but I think that for most, choosing a career is a balance of probabilities and pro/con lists that help you to decide what's best for you in this moment — with a healthy dose of intuition and serendipity added in, of course.

There will always be the "grass is greener on the other side" syndrome. But the key is to recognize that even if one choice is imperfect, there's no perfect choice, you can never have all the information you need to make a perfect decision, and what you've chosen now is what's right for you now because you chose it. It's been said that maybe *you* don't find the right career, that maybe *it* finds you. I guess it depends how much you believe in serendipity and the like. But I think it's a good idea that perhaps the career you end up with is the right one in the universe for you at that time. For example, if you get a certain position but not another, maybe that second one wasn't right for you, anyway. Maybe the position you have is what's right for you now. Maybe you're exactly where you need to be. We only have a limited time on this earth, and finding a great career next step is amazing, to be sure, but spending all your days wondering whether there might be something else that's better isn't the best or most productive way to spend your days.

If you find yourself in this position, try timeboxing your apprehension. Instead of doubting all the time, decide on a time slot, maybe a certain hour per day or an hour per week, if you can manage it, where you worry non-stop. You can wallow in the agonizing, but only for that hour! Then when you find yourself worrying outside that time, because it's bound to happen, stop and remind yourself that you've scheduled your fretting (as laughable as that might sound) and that now isn't the time to be stewing. I find that for many things in life, scheduling is a highly effective answer.

You may read this book and end up considering quitting your job only to find yourself in an abyss of worry, regret, and doubt. I'm not necessarily advocating that. The strategies here can be done in any amount of time, even if you have a full-time job or two full-time jobs. In fact, for some people (many!), it's better to stay in a job and explore your next step on the side rather than investigate your next step full-time. Then at least you have something, and you're not stuck explaining a huge résumé gap to potential employers. But if you do have a big résumé gap, not to worry — there are ways to explain it away.

If you do decide to quit your job, this is your official warning that it might not be the walk in the park you imagined it to be. Sure, it might sound appetizing to spend your days at the beach, having leisurely lunches with friends, or watching Netflix. But what happens when the beach gets cold, all your friends are working so they don't have time to lunch, and you've watched everything on Netflix (if that's even possible)? You're sunk. You might think that would take months or even years to happen, but it's amazing how quickly being sick of unlimited free time can occur, especially if you have a tendency to get sick of *whatever* is happening.

Be honest with yourself about this! I know that I, unfortunately, have a tendency toward dissatisfaction and looking over my shoulder, wondering, *Is this what I should be doing right now?* But the good news is that these days we don't technically need to choose. Today, for many people, there isn't that *one thing* they do day in and day out. Instead, their careers are portfolios of different micro-jobs they perform on different days, on a regular basis, or for short periods of time. Such is the case of freelancers, consultants, or anyone participating in this new work economy, the new way of doing business.

So if you think your ideal day is to go to the beach and watch Netflix (or better yet, do both at once), think again. After a few days or weeks of that, you may start to wonder what you're contributing to society. You may begin to get bored. Your creative muscles might atrophy. You may soon *want* a job. But then when you apply, it could take months to find something. It's not necessarily a matter of weeks — it can take much longer than that. So this is my case for staying in a job until you find another one.

Then there are those of us who feel that the mere existence of a job in our life suffocates us from discovering an alternative, from devoting the mental and physical space to explore, dream, and do. This might be true for some of us. At times I've certainly felt as though it were that way for me. But a good friend pointed out that perhaps that's only a perception of mine, and maybe if I'd stayed in a job, I might have avoided the wallowing and uncertainty that ensued. Yes, it happened to me. It happens to the best of us! But sometimes the difficulties that come with transitions can end up helping us figure out and find something better.

Studies show that after a job loss, mental health issues such as depression are likely to ensue.[10] In many cases, these are temporary. But for others, some can linger. If you find yourself *funemployed*, my best advice is to try to fill your days with activities you've scheduled in your calendar, ideally with other people. Things to look forward to. Things that make it feel less like a big empty open calendar for the rest of your life. You can also establish a "place," somewhere to go to aside from your house to do your job search and exploration. A place with familiar faces — one that feels supportive. This will help replace the sense of community and familiarity you had in your job with your colleagues, at least until you find something new with a new set of awesome people! Looking for work while unemployed can be lonely. If you do get depressed, find a therapist to talk to. If things become dire, call the emergency department. I'm not saying things will get that bad, but I am providing a warning in case they do. It's pretty tricky to go from a lifetime of days programmed by others, whether it be school, a job, whatever, to a long, seemingly endless time in which your days are programmed (or not so programmed) by you.

There, you've been forewarned! Still want to proceed? Then dare to look deep within and see both your flaws and potential for greatness and increased fulfillment.

Life and Career as a Series of Tests

No one can tell you what you should do for the rest of your life. Only YOU can make things happen. But you must take action. You learn best from your own actions, not advice from someone else. You have a lot of good experience. Call up someone you used to work with just to chat. Listen to them. Tell them about yourself. Do it!!! My ideas are in a couple of books: *Luck Is No Accident; Fail Fast, Fail Often.*

— JOHN KRUMBOLTZ,
"Practical Career Counseling Applications
of the Happenstance Learning Theory"[1]

When I first arrived in Silicon Valley, I had the amazing opportunity of meeting with John Krumboltz at Stanford University. John is a sort of "meta" figure in the field of career counselling — he counsels career counsellors on how to do career counselling. When I first learned about him and his work, I was incredibly excited about the possibility of meeting him while in California, and he certainly didn't disappoint. Our hour together exceeded all expectations that I had. John has perspectives on career counselling that are unlike pretty much anything I've ever heard before, but they are the ones that resonate with me the most. What follows are my biggest takeaways from our encounter.

There's no way that you can declare in advance what career is best for you, yet this is the way career counselling is done in most of the world. For example, in Britain, you have to declare what career you'll have for the rest of your life at age 15, and after that, it's very difficult to change. John referenced the example of a guy who had written *chemistry* on the slip of paper given to him at 15 because he'd heard that you could make a lot of money in it. Ten years later, John met him, and having done three degrees in chemistry and finally entering a job in the chemical industry, the man realized he hated it. Yet at 25, he planned to stay in it for the rest of his life, anyway, because of all the time and work he'd put in to get there and how difficult it would be to switch. In my mind, this is a massive tragedy — a young person committing to stay for the rest of his life (or for any length of time, for that matter) in a hated job.

John and I agreed that this sort of career choice would probably lead to many health problems, as I had experienced in my corporate job after only a few months — eye twitches, neck pains, and back problems I'd never had before in my life. We also agreed that ongoing job dissatisfaction could lead to problems with home life, family, and/or relationships. This decision could affect all areas of your life and make you hate everything you do. Think of the potential that would be lost. Imagine what impact you could make if you did what you loved instead.

Krumboltz's perspective was to simply try out some alternatives to see what you like, because you never know what the world will look like a few years from now or what you'll want/like in the future. Don't do something now for the sole purpose of it getting you to something better later, because the world is changing quickly and that thing might not be needed anymore, or you might not even like it when you get to it. In which case, you can choose something else. For example, if I'm interested in becoming a venture capitalist (VC), I might see the steps toward that as working for a consulting firm or investment bank for two years, then doing an M.B.A., then getting a VC job. Well, what if by the time I finished my M.B.A., VCs are no longer needed in the world for some reason, or I get a VC job and hate it? Or maybe by then VC jobs don't require backgrounds in consulting or i-banking and an M.B.A. experience, then no worries. If I hate every minute of those four years, that would be pretty sad. Here are some of John's further thoughts on forging a career:

1. **Focus mainly on what you'd like to do now:** John's method of counselling advises you to make a list of the things you'd most like to try next and then choose what's best from among them. For example, at the moment I would have loved to travel to India and live in an ashram, go to the Start-Up Chile incubator program, do a week at 10 different startups, DJ for a season at a ski resort, et cetera. And at that very moment, I saw spending a week at 10 different startups as the best option. Then he said to figure out the first step toward making that best option happen — in my case, how would I get the people in the first startup to let me shadow them for a week?

2. **Stop thinking/reflecting and just do something:** Learn more by trying/doing things, not by discussing theories or meditating on it. Life is a long series of experiments. John never "decided" to be a college professor, but it was the best among the opportunities available to him at the time, and he loved it so much that he stayed. Start doing something valuable for other people now. Engage in the world in a meaningful way. Try to learn from it and do a good job at it.

3. **Every work experience is valuable:** It's better to have some job than no job, and you can learn a lot even if your job isn't your ideal one. Everything you try is a learning experience, and you shouldn't view the experience or yourself as a failure if you end up not liking it. John referenced my time in the corporate world as a very valuable experience, and I agree. I learned so much about how I did and didn't want to live and what types of work environments I wanted to and didn't want to work in. Had I not had

that experience early in life, I might have made some major bad choices later. John stressed that you can learn a lot from mistakes and therefore it's good to make mistakes.

4. **Avoid overcommitting unnecessarily:** John cautioned me about committing myself to 10 weeks at 10 different startups if I didn't actually need to. I could start with one day or one week, see if it was a good learning experience, then decide if I wanted to stay there, go somewhere else, or stop the experiment altogether. Building on the concept of "minimum viable product" from the startup world, I like this idea of making the minimum viable commitment to an experience, rather than jumping in and committing to a longer amount of time (e.g. a year) without any testing first to see whether I liked it or not. If I were a student doing the corporate job search right now, I'd ask if I could spend at least a day, or even a week, at each of the companies I was considering. I'd do as much prototyping as possible. I'd talk to past and present employees at the companies.

5. **Set a fun limit instead of a time limit:** I asked John what if I spent a few years flitting about to various countries and working for a few months at a time and then no one wanted to hire me because I looked so flighty? Wouldn't my time be better spent working somewhere like Facebook or Google where afterward the job possibilities would be endless? John asked if I'd enjoy working at those places or at the job opportunities that came about after them, and I didn't know the answer to that. He said you shouldn't set a time limit on experiences (e.g. "I will stay here for two years"), but a fun limit. If you're not having fun anymore, then quit. Don't stay in a job you hate just because you're worried it will look bad on your résumé if you leave soon after starting. John said that these days such an idea is a fallacy because people change careers so often. Plus, if you're really worried, you can take it off your curriculum vitae (CV) or only put the year on your CV (rather than also listing the months employed there) and explain it to prospective employers in the interview. Don't be a slave to your CV. Requiring "two years of experience" is a stupid system, and although you do need to adapt

to the stupidity of life in some ways, you can choose to play it like a game. You get success in life by surprising your opponents. For instance, Michael Dell, Steve Jobs, and Bill Gates did this by succeeding despite their college-dropout status. John told me that the world is a crazy place, but you can decide to enjoy it, anyway.

6. **You learn the most through what you do in the real world, not through lectures:** Professors don't necessarily get chosen based on who has the most knowledge of a topic. They often get picked on the basis of whether they have a Ph.D. or not, which doesn't necessarily mean they know more. Therefore, having a Ph.D. is helpful mainly because the "system" says it's valuable. John's view on education is similar to what I've been hearing a lot lately: although having a degree doesn't necessarily mean you know more, the world is structured in such a way that people with more degrees sometimes get more opportunities and more money in jobs. Yet the value of a formal education is grossly overvalued. John emphasized that a degree won't automatically get you a job and that there are lots of unemployed or low-paid master's and Ph.D. graduates out there. Finishing a degree doesn't automatically guarantee success, but dropping out of college doesn't necessarily mean you can't have success (Mark Zuckerberg is another example of this). John said that in order to prototype a potential degree experience, you could talk to current students, attend classes, and think hard about the potential time and cost commitments of removing yourself from the workforce for a few years. He said to be very cautious about committing yourself to it but that you could always drop out. And you won't know if the degree is useful to you until you finish it.

If I boil down John's proposed steps for career transitions into steps, they would be as follows. You'll notice that this is similar to the design process and also to the Lean Startup model promoted by Eric Ries.[2] It's remarkable how many things in life you can apply these ideas to:

- **Ideate:** Make a list of the most fun/awesome/cool/educational experiences available to you.

- **Prototype:** Choose the best option. Figure out how you can make it happen with a minimum viable commitment.
- **Test:** Do it to your fullest ability, try to provide value along the way, and learn as much as you can. If you like it, keep going with it. If it gets boring, learn from the experience and go back to **Ideate**.

Let's put John Krumboltz's tips into action. You might notice that this is also similar to Stanford University's d.school design-thinking process: Empathize > Define > Ideate > Prototype > Test > Repeat.

3 Introducing the Prototyping Your Career Method

Unless you try to do something beyond what you
have already mastered, you will never grow.

— RONALD E. OSBORN

The Prototyping Your Career Method is a new, semi-scientific approach to decision-making. You can apply this process to big career decisions in life, such as choosing your next role, and in one of the last chapters, I share how you can also apply it to other areas of life, such as selecting a new extracurricular activity, neighbourhood, school for your kids, and much more.

In this book, I use a lot of concepts I've learned from the entrepreneurial world such as *lean*, *prototyping*, *minimum viable product*, *pivot*, *hypotheses*, and *validation*. A good deal of the methodology employed in building breakthrough technology startups can be successfully applied to many areas of life, such as romance, day-to-day decisions, and my favourite area to relate it to, career choices. Going forward, I explain each of the aforementioned terms, but if you want to get additional background information, I recommend reading *The Lean Startup* by Eric Ries or checking out *The Four Steps to the Epiphany* by Steve Blank.[1] You can also apply design methodology and think of yourself as the user. High-tech entrepreneurs are the rock stars of our times, and a lot of their methodologies can be applied in a way that improves our lives.

This method applies principles and ideas from the quantified self movement, lean processes, design thinking, startup methodology (e.g. fail fast), the Stanford "Design Your Life" class, the Stanford d.school, the maker movement, amazing companies (e.g. Google), and incredible founders and CEOs (e.g. PayPal co-founder Peter Thiel).

Subsequent chapters in this book explain the key steps that follow. For now, let's do a brief overview of them:

Step 1: Understanding Current Research: To make a decision on a topic, it helps to research what the best practices are. Even if you choose not to apply the research, it's good to know what the thought leaders are currently saying about the topic.

Step 2: Casting a Net: Here, we go as broad as possible to uncover all the different options for your next career move. This process involves two key sub-steps:

- **Know Thyself:** How can you choose what's right for you if you don't know yourself? Or put into design terms, how can you design something for a user you know nothing about? For this sub-step, you use tools and processes to get to know yourself so you can later work toward finding the best next career for you.
- **Know Your Options:** Keeping the theme of going as broad as possible, in this sub-step you come up with all the career options you can possibly dream of. Since this is the brainstorming phase, you won't hold anything back. You come up with many ideas, including some you might never have thought of before, using the research and processes suggested.

Step 3: Narrowing It Down: Of course, there are practicalities associated with career selection. In this step, you identify your practical limitations and narrow your career options slightly based on them. We differentiate between facts and assumptions and ensure that we leave as many viable options available as possible.

Step 4: Career Design Process: A great way to design your career is to follow a design process. In this step, I borrow examples from the best design schools to apply design thinking to my modified process for "designing your career." After step 4, we run through six further steps (4.1 to 4.6) and repeat them as necessary to go from a huge list of possibilities down to three top options to pursue.

Step 4.1: Identify Options: Write out your narrowed-down list of career possibilities as it stands at this moment in time.

Step 4.2: Minimum Viable Commitments (MVCs): Identify ways to learn more about your career options in the most low-commitment ways possible. This limits your time investment while broadening your understanding of options, making it a time-efficient way to try things out. For example, you might decide to do 30 minutes of online research on each of your chosen options.

Step 4.3: Prototype/Test: This is the "trying it out" phase! You go into your online research, informational interviews, et cetera, with an open mind and heart, and participate fully.

Step 4.4: Measure: It's not just experiencing the option that counts; you also need to apply some sort of measurement or rating to later narrow the options you have.

Step 4.5: Narrow: Now for the narrowing process. In this step, you use the criteria you measured previously to narrow your options before moving on and investing more time in the options you've selected.

Step 4.6: Repeat: Now go back to **Identify Options** and begin again! You do this over and over to go from your huge list of options, to less, to three.

* * *

Once you have three ideal options of what you want to do, how do you land one of them? We discuss that in chapter 14, "Your Top Three." Then, once you know what you need to do to succeed, how can you do those things? Chapters 15 and 16 show you how to upgrade your skills and yourself to land that awesome job. But before we move on to the first step in chapter 4, let's define a few of the terms I've mentioned.

Design Thinking: Refers to design-specific cognitive activities that designers apply during the process of designing, i.e., "design as a way of thinking." In practice, I've seen design thinking as a series of steps. As mentioned earlier, at Stanford University's d.school, the steps are Empathize > Define > Ideate > Prototype > Test, e.g. steps to follow to come up with a good product or service solution for a given target market. In chapters 7 to 13, we go through a set of specific steps, many of which relate to the stages in the Stanford d.school model. We design a solution as if designing it for a customer, but in this case the customer is ourselves.

Lean Manufacturing: Sometimes called *lean production* or simply *lean*, this is a systematic method for the elimination of waste within a manufacturing system. *Lean* also takes into account waste created through overburden and waste created through unevenness in work loads. In this process, we work on eliminating waste, in other words, eliminate wasting your time on careers you don't like so that you don't invest too much time in any one career that might not satisfy you at all.

Lean Startup: A practice for developing products and businesses based on "validated learning to get customer feedback quickly and often. The process was proposed by Eric Ries in 2011. The objective is to eliminate uncertainty in the product development process. This is a lean career selection. We work on getting feedback (yours) early and often to validate your interest and strengths in careers. It's meant to decrease your uncertainty regarding your eventual career choice.

Prototyping: In software development, a prototype is a rudimentary working model of a product or information system, usually built for demonstration purposes or as part of the development process. In the Systems Development Life Cycle (SDLC) Prototyping Model, a basic version of the system is built, tested, and then reworked as necessary until an acceptable prototype is finally achieved from which the complete system or product can now be developed. We make prototypes of our potential future career steps, starting with small and rudimentary commitments and experiences that allow us to know whether or not we enjoy the career and whether or not we're good at it before progressing to building larger prototypes until inevitably we develop an acceptable prototype and can then select a final/complete option — at least final for now before our next major career change.

Quantified Self: A movement to incorporate technology into data acquisition on aspects of a person's daily life in terms of inputs (e.g. food consumed, quality of surrounding air), states (e.g. mood, arousal, blood oxygen levels), and performance (mental and physical). In the Career Design Process, step 4 in chapter 7, we incorporate technology (a process) in terms of states (mood) and performance (mental). We measure how we like different careers in order to inform a better selection.

Now let's head to the next chapter and step 1.

Step 1: Understanding Current Research

Just think of happy thoughts and then you'll fly.

— Peter Pan

It's always helpful to begin any quest with serious research, using books, articles, and other forms of research on the topic. In this case, I've done some of the research for you. But it's always good to do more research of your own, e.g. so you're up to date with the latest information. Here's what I've found out concerning careers. I'll explain more about this as we go forward.

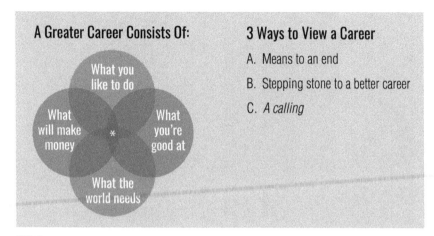

FIG. 3: *What a great career should include and three ways to view it.*

WHAT IS WORK? SHOULD WE WORK? WHY?

It might seem obvious why we should work, but when answering big philosophical questions, I first like to examine the roots of things. In this case, why should we work? To some, work might seem boring and a waste of time. Others might feel as though they're entitled to a guaranteed income from the government. It's my belief that working helps us to self-actualize. It gives us something to do, somewhere to go, something higher than ourselves to commit to. Some people dream of having hours and hours of free time and no work to do, but trust me when I say that if you've never experienced such a state for yourself, it gets old fast.

If you go to somewhere like the Burning Man festival in Nevada, which is entirely participant-driven (people create amazing "art cars," costumes, art decorations, and more for others to enjoy), you'll see that in an event such as that, if one person doesn't contribute, then an aspect of the experience is lost. If no one contributes, there's no experience. In real-world terms, if no one worked, how would we get our vegetables? It would be impossible — *some* people would have to work to help us get them, unless robots did all our work for us, but that's a topic for another book. And if some people have to work, it's only fair that most or all of us work to the best of our ability and to the extent that we can.

Here I count work as productive activities, e.g. that help others. So if you're spending time cooking for your family and cleaning the house, that could still be considered work. It's economically productive and has economic value. If you weren't doing it, your family would need to go out and buy meals and incur additional expenses versus the cost-saving effectiveness of cooking at home. So, to me, work is anything but sitting at home on your keister and staring at the wall, although if it's meditation, that could be considered work, too! So let's refine work as such: any activity that helps others in some way at some point.

What's your unique contribution to the world? What might the world miss if you neglect to provide it? Depending on your spiritual attunement, some people believe we were each put here for a reason, a purpose. And if we don't try to fulfill that mission, have we failed ourselves, failed those around us, and depending on your beliefs, failed whatever higher power might have put us here?

So what's your mission and do you choose to accept it?

One thing to note: believing that each person has *one* mission might seem pretty hard-core and invoke a need to find that perfect career, the one that will help us accomplish what we were put on earth to do. But that type of thinking can lead to a lot of wheel-spinning and indecisiveness, so I argue that we each have *multiple* missions we can pursue, and some of us go after one and some seek more than one. This definition is for no other reason than to inspire *action*, to encourage choice.

TELL ME MORE

To get a good career fit, I believe you need certain elements (think of them in a pyramid as in Abraham Maslow's hierarchy of needs): first, confidence at the base, then skills and knowledge (including self-knowledge), then opportunities. No job is perfect, and everyone has a different definition of what an ideal career looks like. Every job can have value — we all provide services and products to other people. To be honest, I admit I have a personal bias against people selling cigarettes or weapons. But other than that, anything goes! I think jobs should add value to other people, but the definition of this can be vague. You might add value by being a sports star.

At Burning Man, everyone offers something, and that makes up the experience. People create art cars, experiences, costumes, and gifts to give to their fellow "burners." It's a beautiful cornucopia of offerings, and the event wouldn't be what it is without them. In my camp, we were encouraged to think about what our highest point of contribution to the event would be and then offer it. The result was singers singing, dancers dancing, and people using hidden talents they might not normally exercise. When I walk around a neighbourhood and look at the stores and shop owners, I think of it much like Burning Man, where everyone offers what they can to fellow citizens. We all ideally try to figure out what we can do to add the most value to others and then do it. Adding more value usually means making more happiness for yourself, and making more money. And doing something you also love and are good at often means making even more happiness for yourself, and even more money.

Here are some stories of people who were in less-than-ideal job situations who now are doing something they like better. All names have been changed.

Josie was working in investment banking, and she hated it. Now she's a hairdresser and loves what she does. Every day she wakes up excited to go to work because she wants to be creative and help people feel more confident. At home, she has a dog and child. While she isn't exactly rolling in cash, she has enough to get by, and she's happier with that than making more money in a job she doesn't like. She has the flexibility to take time off when she wants to. And one day she might even open her own studio.

Mike was a starving actor who was unhappy. Now he's a corporate lawyer. He loves what he does because he gets to help startups. Every day he's learning and growing, and as a long-time lover of rules and order, he gets to flex his skills in those areas to help people succeed. He makes a great deal of money, and while there are a lot of corporate politics to deal with, he's willing to put up with that in exchange for the benefits he gets from the job. As a young single male, he's fine working long hours.

WHAT'S IN A CAREER?

My view of a career is similar to my take on climbing a mountain. You can train for it, but you never know whether or not the training you've done is adequate until you actually start climbing. You can think you know which path is best for you, but then you realize it leads to a dead end and you need to switch to a different path. Or you can just change routes because you realize you might like another one better. You can either train to climb the mountain and then tackle it when you're ready or take the escalator to the top and skip the training part, but that might have consequences later. Or you might decide to choose a different mountain entirely. Most importantly, in terms of what I'm trying to get across with this book, you can begin to figure out which mountain or path is best for you by testing a number of them. Only once you've given them a try can you really know which one will be best for you. You can always predict and pontificate about which career you think will be best for you, but until you're actually in the thick of it giving it a shot from day to day, you'll never know.

Keep in mind that if you're feeling unhappy in life or at work, it doesn't mean your career is to blame. Many people make the mistake of thinking their careers are the be-all and end-all, but really they're just pieces, parts of life, pie slices that help add up to a whole. And if you're unhappy at work, it could be because you're unhappy at home and your feelings from home are seeping into your work. The single biggest predictor of happiness is the strength and depth of your human relationships. So, if you're unhappy, how are your relationships looking?

Work can help to a point — finding workmates to talk to, for instance — but the most in-depth and fulfilling relationships you'll have are probably outside work, e.g. with family, friends, romantic relationships, or children. That being said, it's a double-edged sword because being happier can help you develop better relationships. So it's the age-old question: Is it the chicken or the egg? Maybe it's that you're looking at work in the wrong way. Even work that may not necessarily be seen as glamorous can lead to job satisfaction — especially if the purpose of it is personally viewed by the worker as profound, and they believe they're serving others and making their lives better. And they're right! Similar to my reasons for writing this book, I believe that a successful career is one that makes the life of at least *one* person better. And it might just be that it makes your life better. But ideally, it makes your life better and at least one *other* person's life better. This purpose will help you get through the thick and thin of things.

We can view work in one of three ways:

- A means to an end, e.g. a way to get money in order to spend time with your family and buy resources. In this view, the job being enjoyable is a bonus but by no means a requirement. Some people view a job as a human being saying, "I'll give you X amount of money to do Y tasks." In this scenario, a person gives you money and in exchange you do work. Then, with your money, you can partially employ other people, e.g. when you buy a shirt you're contributing to the wages of those who made that shirt.

- A stepping stone to a better job, e.g. "I'm articling so I can become a lawyer," "I'm working an entry-level job so I can move up and get a better-paying job." The tricky thing with this viewpoint is that things always change. While being an accountant might once have to led to being a CEO, things might change and evolve over time and suddenly that's no longer the case. So if you're going into medical school to make a good salary as a doctor, keep in mind that, depending on your country, the government could easily claw back on a doctor's wages before you graduate, leading you to make much less than you anticipated. That being said, things can also swing the other way. A dry-cleaning job might not seem so glamorous now, but maybe there will be an opportunity for you to start or join a dry-cleaning franchise. Did you know that dry-cleaning franchises have been said to be the type of franchise most likely to make someone a millionaire?[1] That's right. The person providing you with clean clothes might just be a millionaire.

- A calling, e.g. a part of your life you were meant to do, your contribution to the world. Some of the most successful people with the biggest purpose and impact don't want to stop working; they work so hard because they feel as if they're making a difference every day with their business/work.[2]

In case it wasn't already obvious, I view work as a calling.

There are two parts to work: process and outcome. Outcome is what happens as a result of your work — salary, impact, et cetera. Process is what you do to get to that outcome; it's the day-to-day work. It's my belief that both the process and the outcome of a given career step should be exciting and important for you, not one or the other. And if you improve and focus on the process, it can lead to a better outcome.

"We become what we do" is a statement I heard in one of the classes I audited at Stanford University. It was in reference to the fact that many graduates choose to do something to make lots of money and then plan something more altruistic later. Trouble is, many of them never end up moving to the altruistic plan. "After I get this promotion" becomes "After I buy my house" becomes regrets on their deathbed that they never did what they said they would do. The key is to choose something that allows you to look back after three, five, ten, or more years and be happy with what you did. Maybe it wasn't what you'd choose again, but at least it was the best choice you could make with the knowledge you had at the time. After all, none of us know how long we have left to live — so let's live as if today could be our last day.

YOUR GUIDING STAR

I believe that the best type of work for someone sits at the intersection of, in no particular order:

1.   What you love to do.
2.   What you're good at.
3.   What helps the world.
4.   What makes you money.[3]

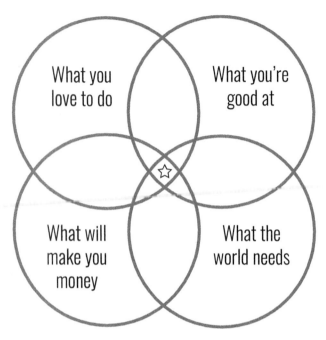

FIG. 4: *Your guiding star for the best career.*

You can see this intersection in the diagram above via the star, your "guiding star," as I like to call it.

If you get the four things in the diagram right, you can't miss embarking on the next awesome career step. Let's break down each element of the diagram and examine them in detail.

The Case for What You Love to Do

It might sound weird, but there are people who don't think work is something to be enjoyed. "That's why they call it a job," I've heard people say. For something that occupies a huge portion of our waking hours (e.g. 36 percent if you work 40 hours a week and sleep eight hours a night), it seems bizarre to me that people are willing to accept doing something they don't enjoy, or even something they hate. When you're doing something you like, you're happier, more productive, and can even live longer.

At the opposite end of the spectrum, doing something you hate can lead to all sorts of health problems.

I once said to my doctor something along the lines of "I'm really enjoying my job. It feels weird. Maybe it's too easy and I should do something else." It's as if we're bred to believe work is hard, that work requires suffering. But suffering can be optional. Just because I'm enjoying work doesn't mean I need to change jobs. Isn't work supposed to be enjoyable — maybe not always, but at times? If you've found something enjoyable, there's little point in switching to something you enjoy less. Why would you? Some people might feel it's a badge of honour to do something they dislike, adding to the litany of conversations of those who say how they hate their jobs, hate their bosses, whatever. Certainly, doing something you dislike helps you to fit in, since you'll be joining the 80 percent of people doing the same, but why not be a beacon of light? If you feel awkward sticking out like a tall poppy, don't worry; there's no need to brag and shout from the rooftops about how awesome your new job is. You can have quiet enjoyment if that makes you feel more comfortable. Although I prefer to think it can be helpful to encourage more people to join the like-your-work revolution.

That being said, work isn't always a walk in the park. Work isn't designed to make you happy while you sit back, cruise, and lap up the benefits. Doing anything worthy or world-changing can have struggles that come along with it. The key is managing through those struggles and knowing that your work is worth it. For more on this, check out books such as *The Obstacle Is the Way*[4] or *Life Is in the Transitions*.[5]

The Case for What You're Good At

Choosing something easy or hard? How about something that's both — it comes naturally to you but there are stretch challenges. Playing to your strengths can yield immense results; it helps you be more successful and feel more at ease. Plus, if we're aiming to help the world as much as possible (and help ourselves, via compensation), why wouldn't we pick one of the things we're best at? Check out a book like *Strengths Finder 2.0* to back this up with real data.[6]

The Case for What Helps the World

Life is like a loan given from God, or whatever higher power or science you believe in, so give it back with interest. If you only worry about your own well-being, that's selfish and unfulfilling. Working on a cause greater than yourself can boost happiness. And I believe it's the responsible thing to do. When countries start to run out of water, it boggles my mind how people can decide to devote time to launching the next brand of sugary candy snacks. Instead of thinking, "What can I get?" think, "What can I *give*?" It will come back to you in spades. It's a powerful mindset, one that I believe ends up in more personal material success, anyway. Also, the less you focus on yourself, the less stress you'll experience. An intense focus on yourself can create a boatload of stress.

If you have a religious or spiritual inclination, you might believe, as I do, that we were put on earth to *serve*. Plus, when you look at yourself in the mirror every day or tell other people what you do, what's going to make you feel better, selling tobacco or helping entrepreneurs get microloans? There are plenty of social entrepreneurs, companies with social-impact objectives (e.g. B Corporations), and purpose-driven firms in general that you could join. And these days you can still make a lot of money while doing good for the world!

All that aside, I do believe there's inherent value to most types of work, even if it isn't the most impact-driven. Some people ask questions like "Why am I worthy?" and to me, the answer is "Because you're human." I believe a similar answer exists for careers. The question "Why is your work valuable?" is answered by "Because it's work." Any work can be valuable, to the extent that it helps you and ideally helps others. Of course, I would discourage careers that involve something illegal or immoral, but aside from that, many things can be argued to be positive.

The Case for What Makes You Money

We all need to eat. Seriously, I don't believe there's any glory in depriving yourself of a salary. It's all a matter of personal opinion, but mine is that you can help others more when you have adequate resources to support and nourish yourself. I'm not saying you need to do what makes the *most* money; after all, that might be incompatible with what you like to do or what you're good at. But I believe you should try to make a living wage such that you're self-reliant and don't need to live off your parents or anyone else, unless there are extenuating circumstances or you've worked out some sort of mutually agreeable scenario, e.g. you do all the housework while your partner goes out and works. It's an interesting fact that above $75,000 in income, additional increases in income haven't been proven to materially impact happiness.[7] What we call success is sometimes in direct opposition to what really makes us happy — connections to others. And by the way, use of social networking websites is a paltry substitute for in-person connection. It's unfulfilling and unsatisfactory.

The Interplay

Maybe there's something you love, but you're not good at it. Maybe you're great at something, but you can't stand doing it. These sorts of paradoxes are both what makes decisions hard and what makes life fun. You need to decide which criteria is the highest priority for you. For me, it's doing something that I like. Everything else falls in line after that. But the answer may be different for you.

The Best Step for *Now*

You might be looking for a cosmic sign that this is the right career for you. Maybe you'll come across one, but there's a good chance you won't. Does that mean you shouldn't make a change? I don't believe so. I've come to think that a decision will probably never feel *perfect*, probably because there's no such thing as perfect. It may feel risky and scary, but if it's the right decision, ideally it will feel like the best choice out of the set of options you have. Also, once you're in the career, it might still not seem like the right decision. There might be a ton of doubt. It might only be in the future looking back that your series of career choices makes sense to you.

The Conclusion for *Now*

Find what you love and put your whole heart into it. Here's something to read that you might find useful: *Jonathan Livingston Seagull* by Richard Bach, a book about a seagull who wants something more than the daily grind of his food-focused seagull friends.[8] I believe finding a career that works better for you is much like this — it's flying to new heights.

5 Step 2: Casting a Net

> You can't connect the dots looking forward; you can only connect them looking backward. So you have to trust that the dots will somehow connect in your future. You have to trust in something — your gut, destiny, life, karma, whatever.
>
> — STEVE JOBS

Based on my experience with a corporate job, I realized that no one was going to tell me what job to do to make me happy. And no one but me could even know the answer to that question. I was going to have to figure that out on my own. I'd done all the supposedly right things to help me select the corporate job — career testing, talking to guidance counsellors, speaking to people in the field, reading about the subject online — but clearly it hadn't worked. It was time to take matters into my own hands. It was time to figure out who I was and who I wanted to be. This is my process — but you might make your own. Hopefully, in either case, learning about my process is helpful to you in that you can follow mine or create your own.

In my mind, the first step to making a next career move you'll love is to cast a wide net. What does that mean? Like a fisherman, you're going to try to catch all the fish you can. What I mean by this is that you'll work on finding all the career opportunities that *could* be a fit. Instead of going deep on a handful of options right away, you'll work on a shallow dive into *many* different opportunities at first. This helps mitigate the chance of missing something awesome. Of course, no one can ever claim to know about *every* career opportunity that exists, but it can be helpful to know a bunch! Did you know that on average most kids can only name six different types of careers? Yet plenty of more options exist than your standards: doctor, lawyer, accountant, firefighter, nurse, teacher, et cetera. And depending on where you live and what you've been exposed to, there might be many careers out there that could be a great fit for you that you've never heard of. There are literally thousands of career options out there.

How are you going to do this? In this chapter, you will learn about tools and questions you can ask yourself to help you move along this process. You work on *broadening* yourself and your options. Later, we work on narrowing. But before we even get into identifying careers, we deal with something ultra important that many people often neglect to think about when searching for a job: *getting to know yourself.*

KNOW THYSELF

How can you choose a job that's a good fit for you if you don't know yourself? It's like trying to fit two puzzle pieces together, but one of the pieces is just a square with no holes to fit the other piece into. You might think as you read this, *Hey, I know myself! Who are you to say I don't?* But do you *really*? If I asked you what you stand for in life, what your purpose is, what your core values are, and what you're willing to accept versus not accept, could you answer those questions? Most people can't answer them. But I'm going to propose, no, *insist*, that it's vital for you to figure out your own answers in order to find a great next career fit.

If you already have all this stuff figured out, congratulations! This chapter will be a review for you, but it will still be helpful to go through to make sure you can succinctly answer these questions for yourself or others, to make certain they're answers you *know* and *feel* rather than answers you read in a book somewhere or answers someone gave you. In this chapter, you'll find a list of soul-searching questions to help prompt you in figuring out your answers to these critical decisions. But first, here's an introduction to some of the tools you'll use to get to know yourself better and answer these questions.

Twelve Tools to Know Thyself

Here are the top tools to help you get to know yourself. We'll get into these in more detail later in this chapter.

1. Journal Writing.
2. Alone Time.
3. Digital Detox.
4. Substance Detox.
5. Meditation.
6. 360-Degree Review.
7. Personality Tests.
8. Counsellors and Coaches.
9. Books, Articles, and Videos
10. Balance.
11. To-Do List.
12. Know Thyself Questions.

Let's get into each of the tools one by one.

Tool No. 1: Journal Writing

Ever written in a journal? Many people used to when they were young but never did again. Some, especially those in the digital generation, have never written in a journal. But writing in a journal can help you learn about yourself. Research has shown that journal writing can reduce stress and increase self-confidence.[1] And it's a great way to organize your thoughts. A great book that references key tips and tricks for keeping a journal is *The Artist's Way* by Julia Cameron, which recommends writing "morning pages," three pages of continuous writing of whatever comes to mind as soon as you wake up in the morning.[2] Whether you do it in the morning or at night, writing in a journal can help you with the all-important task of learning more about yourself. It allows you to spot patterns, identify repeated thoughts that might be negative, and see blocks — which is the first step to overcoming them. A journal also assists in completing get-to-know-you exercises from this book and others.

I've been keeping a journal on and off for years, and within the past year, I've kept one quite regularly and have really felt a positive difference in my life as a result. A psychiatrist I know told me that for many people, writing morning pages can make the difference between feeling off-kilter and staying on track and help you be in control of your life — as if you have a plan, as if you're making progress and getting things done. Paul Graham, the co-founder of at Y Combinator, says:

> "Always produce" is also a heuristic for finding the work you love. If you subject yourself to that constraint, it will automatically push you away from things you think you're supposed to work on, toward things you actually like. "Always produce" will discover your life's work the way water, with the aid of gravity, finds the hole in your roof.[3]

You might still doubt the power of a journal, but think about the power words can have, the power people give to words, and how words can influence lives, sometimes without people even knowing it. I believe that communication is one of the most powerful ways to make a difference in this world. For example, when people feel sad or upset, or don't know what to do regarding certain decisions they have to make, what do they do to try to get through it? Most people I know use a combination of talking to friends and family, going to therapy, and reading articles and/

or self-help books. And all of these things involve words! Words are the way we assign meaning to things in life.

Without getting overly philosophical, I realized after people started emailing me about how my *Forbes* article motivated them to make major changes in their lives, that something as simple, small, and sometimes thoughtless as an article can have real power on the way people lead their lives. And it can have a ripple effect. People read a book or an article and make changes. Then they tell their friends and their friends make changes. Then those friends tell more friends, and so on. It can happen the same way with a product, a song, a type of food, a spiritual way of being, and more. But the way most of these ideas get transmitted is through words. What power! So, as we can see in the case of folks such as former U.S. president Barack Obama, the best communicator often wins. So it makes sense to practise your communication skills and use words to change your life and the lives of others.

Reading articles or books and talking with friends or family involve external people's words, but what about your own words? Find a notebook you love to write in, as well as a pen you love to write with. If you're like me and you view fancy-looking journals as "too nice to write in" and worry about making mistakes and wasting pages, buy a cheap journal. Anything will do as long as it makes you happy.

I use Moleskine Cahier Journals (Large, Plain, Kraft Brown, and Soft Cover, in case you're curious), which come in sets of three. They're the perfect size to fit in my purse (five by eight and a quarter inches), they're plain rather than lined so I can doodle and draw all I want, and they're thin and small so I can carry one for work and one for personal life. As well, their soft cardboard-looking covers make them seem like draft notebooks, reminding me that all of life is a draft and making the notebooks less precious for me to write in. I can write in a Moleskine all I want and not feel guilty using up a fancy notebook quickly, because it isn't super fancy. It's affordable and lies flat, making it easy to use. Plus, you can easily label the front of them. I'm not getting any money from Moleskine for this, I swear. I just love the company's notebooks and have always been somewhat of a stationery aficionado.

Another journal tool I love is *The Five-Minute Journal* (see fiveminute journal.com).[4] Co-created by my friend UJ Ramdas and recommended by the illustrious author and entrepreneur Tim Ferriss, *The Five-Minute Journal* is just what it sounds like — a journal that helps you capture the key elements of your day in five minutes or less. The sections include a gratitude portion (listing what you're grateful for has been proven to increase happiness and well-being),[5] reflections on how you can make your day great, affirmations, and thoughts on how you can make your day better.

I've been using *The Five-Minute Journal* for a while now and find it incredibly helpful and joy-inspiring. It's also a great way to dip your toe into longer journal writing. If the previous comment about morning pages got you thinking, *Three pages on a daily basis! I don't have time for that*, then *The Five-Minute Journal* may be what you need. It will help you identify patterns, see what you love most, and prompt decisions to improve your days. And you know what they say: improve your day, improve your life.

Self Authoring (selfauthoring.com), a series of online writing programs, is also an interesting journal project. Called "The writing assignment that changes lives," it provides tons of prompts to help you answer deep questions in your journal, identify strengths and weaknesses, and more.

Keeping a journal is a great way to reflect on how much you enjoy certain activities. It allows you to turn up the volume of your own thoughts and opinions and turn down the volume of those of others. More knowledge of yourself makes you less susceptible to merely going along with what everyone else is doing. It's important to build your own definition of success rather than trying to live someone else's, because even if they have a definition of success for themselves, they're different than you and therefore it may not work for you. Journal writing is the best way I've found to literally be the author of your own life.

Tool No. 2: Alone Time

I'm constantly amazed by how little alone time some people have told me they've had. Answers ranging from "30 minutes per day" to "none" have got me wondering if we're suffering from some sort of alone-time deprivation.

Now I'm not suggesting you spend your whole life alone. That would defeat the purpose of, well, a lot of things. But spending time alone and quietly is a critical task that shouldn't escape your list, especially while in the process of getting to know yourself. A Google search of *no quiet alone time* yields many academic articles calling for a return to a time when importance was placed on the concept of being alone, and when the idea of solitude was more important. Leo Babauta, author of the blog *Zen Habits* (if you haven't checked it out, I highly recommend it), calls solitude the number one habit of highly creative people (see zenhabits.net/creative-habit). You could also take a look at Babauta's book *Essential Zen Habits*.[6]

If you're not used to spending time alone, it can take a while to get accustomed to it. You might find yourself feeling lonely or wondering why it is even important. You might think, *I learn best through talking to other people.* While that could be the case, it's also important to listen to your own voice solo. It could be saying things you didn't expect to hear.

Finding half an hour or more here and there to be alone is critically important. It could be over your lunch hour. It could mean waking up super early while everyone else is still asleep, or conversely, staying up late after others have gone to bed. Even if you're able to find 10 minutes here and there, it can make a big difference. I find my alone time in a closed room, and if there are sounds, I block them with a white noise machine or noise-cancelling headphones. I also go on solo walks and find this to be quite refreshing. Another amazing thing to do is solo trips, as close as camping in your backyard or as far-flung as going overseas to a foreign country alone.

What should you do or think about while alone? Well, I find it's best just to let your mind wander. It will tell you what it needs to think about. You can also spend this alone time writing in a journal, meditating, and/or thinking about the "big questions" — perhaps some of the ones outlined later in this chapter.

Critically important to alone time is the next tool. Turning off your phone and TV will help ensure you're truly alone — but not in a scary way! I count internet, TV, books, and even music (especially vocal) to be like having someone with you — it's someone else's voice, a distraction from your own thoughts. Tuning out of the external and tuning into yourself can be very powerful.

Tool No. 3: Digital Detox

As smartphones have become more prevalent, many of us feel as if we're "always on," and indeed, our online profiles always are (too bad there isn't a "go to sleep" function for our Facebook profiles). While the internet and all that it's provided in terms of technological advances are tremendous, too much of a good thing can be bad. I've found that extreme power can result from taking a digital detox. It's something I try to do at least four times a year for a couple of days at a time. I also try to spend most of my Sundays off-line. A bit of an extremist, I've now been experimenting with not having internet at my house or on my phone, and this is a change I think I'll stick with. Having my mornings and evenings internet-free really helps me to set up for the day and to wind down. And my friends and colleagues know to contact me by phone if something is urgent.

When you're online, it feels like *zap, zap, zap!* There's all this new information coming at you, and it's literally limitless — except for the limits worldwide servers have, but they're pretty big indeed. Your brain is running in high gear (and it can be literally exhausting), and turning the incoming pings off is literally like coming down from a high. Facebook's notification system is very similar to the most addictive form of gambling, a slot machine. It's variable timing (you never know when you'll get a "win," or in this case a like or mention), and variable reward level (you don't know how much of a reward, or nice a message, you'll get). You get a dopamine hit each time you get a like or a message, which reinforces the behaviour of checking and refreshing. When rats were introduced to a system like that (variable timing and variable reward level) and pressed a lever, they sometimes got a treat and sometimes didn't, so they literally pushed the lever continuously for hours on end. Sound familiar? If that sounds like you, it can be hard to snap out of such a state, but it's all-important to do so to maintain balance and sanity.

Studies have shown that heavy Facebook usage can induce depression.[7] I still use Facebook, but sparingly, and mainly in order to set up times to connect with people in real life. It seems as though humans have created tons of awesome technology, but our brains haven't really kept up and figured out how to effectively deal with all the technology. A digital detox can help.

To aid in the digital detox, I actually attended some summer camps for adults where you checked your phones in at the door. These weren't the types of camps where you went if you "had a problem," though some of the attendees confessed they did. Instead, the camps are a light-hearted and fun time and aimed at reconnecting with how life was as a child. I went to Camp Grounded in California (campgrounded.org), for example. It was an amazing, life-altering experience in which I got to know myself better and discovered more about my capabilities and strengths. It was also a great way to meet people, free of device-checking and selfies. We played "Capture the Flag," stargazed, and roasted marsh-mallows in the moonlight. And we did improv, another awesome way to get to know yourself and others. If you get the chance to attend one of these camps, I highly recommend it. Another great event is Burning Man, which I've already mentioned. Suffice to say that it's a wonderful experience regardless of your level of interest or disinterest in substances.

If you want to be hard-core about it, as alluded to earlier, you can also resist books, TV, and maybe even music during your digital detox. Perhaps you might even take a break from speaking to people. I once stayed at a friend's place in Switzerland alone for a few days and de-cided to do a total detox — no inflow, only outflow. By that I mean no inflow of information or talking, only outflow of my thoughts. The fact that the dominant language there wasn't English really helped! I spent five days not talking to anyone except to order food, not surfing the internet, not watching TV or listening to music, and not reading. Okay, I cracked on the last one in the last day or so — what can I say? I love reading! But I spent the majority of my time thinking and writing. And that time was really powerful for me. I ended up writing some poems, which I hadn't really done since I was a teen, then realized the poems looked an awful lot like songs. So I strung them together to form the basis of a musical I later wrote and produced. Prior to that, I hadn't really written any theatre at all. But it turned out to be one of the most enjoyable experiences of my life! And it was listening to myself and exploring via writing that got me there.

Tool No. 4: Substance Detox

Along the lines of a digital detox, you could also consider a substance detox. Some of you might think, *How is this going to help me get to know myself better?* But once you're off coffee, for example, it's really interesting to track the things you're naturally engaged by without the artificial inducement of caffeine. You can also see which activities make you most tired. Temporary elimination of alcohol can also be enlightening, helping you see which types of people you're most comfortable around, which activities you still enjoy sober, and what social risks you're still willing to take in the absence of "liquid confidence." As for me, I stopped drinking a couple of years ago as an experiment and realized I had more fun and was more engaged when I was sober than when I was drinking. Along the way, I've learned a lot about myself.

Tool No. 5: Meditation

If you're not too detoxed already from tools no. 3 and 4, there's something else you can detox — your brain! Meditation is an increasingly popular activity to do, and it's no wonder why. Studies have shown that meditation actually creates changes in your brain and can lead to increased happiness.[8] There's a growing body of evidence that meditation is just as important as physical exercise, flexibility, and the like. It can also be a great tool to get to know yourself and is a great activity to do during alone time.

Some people don't meditate because they think it's too hard or "don't know how to do it." But it's as simple as closing your eyes and sitting quietly. There's a misconception that if you have a thought, that's bad, and some people complain they "can't stop thinking." But thinking is okay — during your first few sessions, you'll be thinking a lot. But once you've done it for a period of time, you can start working on trying to see the thoughts come up and then watch them slide away without any disappointment on your end for having the thought in the first place.

If you want to take a class, there are free meditation ones in most major cities through an organization called Sri Chinmoy (srichinmoycentre.org). There are also apps such as Headspace (headspace.com) that offer guided meditations you can do at home or on the go (sometimes I like to meditate on the subway). If you want to take a deeper dive, there are 10-day Vipassana silent meditation retreats (dhamma.org), though I don't recommend this until you've had some experience with meditation already, since 10 days of silence and sitting can be intense on the body and mind.

Tool No. 6: 360-Degree Review

Early in my career, I was lucky enough to participate in the Corporate Athlete Training Program. As part of this, we used a tool from the training to conduct a 360-degree review about ourselves from our peers, family members, bosses, and subordinates. The questions asked ranged from "Is the person excited about their work?" to "Do they get enough sleep?" While ultimately I believe that the answers to important questions in your life need to come from you — since no one has your unique profile, they can't decide what's best for you — soliciting feedback from others can be quite powerful, especially when it's done in a systematic way. In my case, the system sent out detailed numeric surveys to the email addresses I put into the software and gave me back anonymized results. The conclusions were incredibly life-changing for me. Each person surveyed reported that I seemed disengaged with my job and that I talked about it a lot. They suggested that it was tiring to hear about, and that if I didn't like it, I should make a change.

This realization struck me hard. My dissatisfaction wasn't just affecting *me*; it was affecting those I cared about and my relationships to them. It was then that I realized that I *must* make a change. When they asked us to write ourselves a letter to receive at our desks in three months, my letter read: "You won't receive this letter because you won't be working here anymore." While some may think this was a waste of training dollars, since I ended up leaving my job partly as a result of it, I think it's good to weed out the dissatisfied employees early. Dissatisfied employees can be very costly to an organization. It's great if your review can also include information about what people think you like most, what they think you're best at, et cetera.

A friend of mine, Kevin Rustagi, sent out a Google Survey to a number of his friends and colleagues as part of his Reputation Management class at Stanford University, taught by JD Schramm and Allison Kluger. He emailed all of us the following:

> Hi everyone!
>
> You're receiving this because I trust you and we've known each other for some time. I'm gathering totally anonymous data on how I'm perceived for the final project in my Reputation Management class. To do so, I've made a 5-question survey that should take ~2 min. (Trying to get all responses by Tuesday eve as I'm completing the project this week.)
>
> Hope that this finds you well — and thank you!!!
>
> <Name>
>
> PS. Staying in <City> the coming year <insert upcoming career plans here>. Hit me up when you're out here and/ or whenever!

When I clicked through to the link, here's what I found:

<Name>'s Anonymous Reputation Survey

I really, really, really want you to be candid. Trust me — this is anonymous. Brevity totally acceptable.

1. Gender?
    a. Male
    b. Female
    c. Prefer not to disclose

2. How do we (most) know each other?
    a. Work
    b. School
    c. Social
    d. Other

3. In 1–3 words, how would you describe me?

4. What do I do well?

    (On my best day? As few words as you like.)

5. What can I work on?

    (On my worst day? Again, feel free to say as little or as much as you like.)

6. What is something about me that has stayed with you (good, bad, or otherwise)?

    (Feel free to write one thing, or multiple — memories and stories, however brief, are super helpful. Again, this is totally anonymous.)

7. Who am I interested in more? (Circle one.)

    Myself   1   2   3   4   5   6   7   8   9   10   Others

8. Anything else about how you/others perceive me? (Optional.)

THANK YOU!!!

For filling out my survey! ALL feedback is helpful — regardless of what you wrote, I am so grateful.

Then he sent out the following follow-up email:

> Hi everyone!
>
> To those who've filled out my Anonymous Reputation
> Survey, Thank You!!! I've already received such insightful
> and valuable comments and ideas. This has already been
> a wonderful learning experience. Again, this is for a class
> project on our own reputations — where we've been
> and where we'd like to go. Totally Anonymous.
>   For those of you who haven't gotten a chance yet and
> would like to have their feedback heard, I'm closing the
> survey tomorrow, Wednesday, at 7:00 p.m. PST.
>   Thanks again for being so helpful,
>
> <Name>
>
> P.S. If you're curious about the history of this kind
> of 360-degree feedback, see (en.wikipedia.org/
> wiki/360-degree_feedback).

I found this process to be fantastic! That's why I'm featuring it in my book. I'm planning to run it for myself soon, too. And best of all, it's free! Why not do it? It can be scary to get feedback from people, but if you adopt a growth mindset and remember that feedback is a gift and that you can change anything about yourself, you'll realize that it's all good!

Tool No. 7: Personality Tests

Are you an INTP? ENTJ? If this sounds like gobbledygook to you, that's because you haven't taken the Myers-Briggs personality test (myersbriggs .org). This and other personality tests can give you some guidance on how you rank on certain dimensions compared to other people. Although these tests can never be 100 percent accurate — and in some cases are outdated with the list of potential jobs that are available, e.g. social media specialist is probably not on there — they give you a guideline to go off of rather than having just completely blank space/white sky. They won't give you *the answer* of what to do with your career (perhaps there's no *one* answer only; there could be multiple options, like a choose-your-own-adventure book!) and should only be used as a guideline, but they're a good start. Myers-Briggs measures on four dimensions: introverted/extroverted, intuitive/sensing, thinking/feeling, and perceiving/judging. It gives a description of personality types and provides job recommendations. The test is a useful tool for getting to know yourself, and it's fun to ask friends and new romantic prospects, "So, what Myers-Briggs type are you?"

Another personality test I've found useful is the Strong Interest Inventory (cpp.com/products/strong/index.aspx). As its website states, *"The Strong Interest Inventory*® assessment is one of the world's most widely respected and frequently used career planning tools." I went through this testing when I was in high school, and it output a big list of my strongest interests and potential careers. My top match was religious leader. That's not what I'm pursuing now, but I am pursuing a collection of the interests that it recommended.

The CliftonStrengths Assessment (gallup.com/cliftonstrengths/en/home.aspx) is another great test, with a book companion. It can help identify your top strengths (e.g. Activator, Ideator) and provide suggestions on how to apply them to your life and career. Another one is the VIA Signature Strengths Survey (authentichappiness.sas.upenn.edu/testcenter).

Helen Fisher's Chemistry Test (chemistry.com) is a romance test rather than a career test, but it can still be useful in getting to know yourself. The test will help you answer whether you're a Director, Builder, Negotiator, or Explorer and what type(s) you get along with best.

The Hermann Brain Dominance Instrument (HBDI) (herrmannsolutions.com) purports to help you recognize the thinking preferences you have and can be particularly useful in comparing results with team members to help facilitate conversations and teamwork. Insights Discovery (insights.com/564/insights-discovery.html) is a great test, too. Another test you can try is Enneagram (enneagraminstitute.com).

As you can see, there are many personality tests to choose from. Check out which one(s) resonate with you most, or just do them all! It can be helpful to go over the results with a career coach. I met with David Lawson (lawsoncareersolutions.ca), and he helped me interpret the results of the tests and create actionable next steps. Which leads us to the next tool ...

Tool No. 8: Counsellors and Coaches

It can be helpful to talk things out. Speaking to a career counsellor, therapist, psychologist, psychiatrist, or life coach is a rare opportunity to talk about yourself with no expectation of reciprocation. In other words, you can talk about yourself for an hour without feeling guilty not asking anything about the other person. This is an interesting opportunity for self-reflection because a good helping professional will be a mirror reflecting back to you, merely acting as a person for you to talk to and repeating back to you what you've said. They won't make decisions for you but will prompt you to make decisions based on the information you've provided. The theory here is that the answer is already *in you*; it just needs to be tapped into and revealed. I believe this wholeheartedly. When talking to others, it's easy to get into the cycle of thinking you need to keep asking and asking and finally someone will give you the answer of what to do and it will feel right. But in my opinion, that day might never come. So all you can do is pick the best option of the options in front of you and pursue that. But talking to a helping professional can be valuable. And who knows, perhaps they'll point out some unhealthy thinking patterns you could work on to fix. Last time I checked, one in four people have mental health diagnoses.[9] In any case, we make a practice of getting our bodies checked, so why not also get our brains examined? And regardless of whether or not you have a formal diagnosis, if therapy works for you, use it! There's no need to be embarrassed — so many people see therapists these days. In my view, if something's helpful to you, as long as it's not illegal and not going to hurt anyone, you should use it! It could be a competitive advantage for you. If you can't afford this and can't find a free opportunity to talk to someone, you can always enlist the services of a friend to ask you questions and stay silent so he or she can reflect things back to you. You could even find a mentor and/or a mentee. Paradoxically,

I find that giving advice helps me to figure out my own thoughts and give myself advice! But it's more ideal to find a helping professional so you can take a no-holds-barred approach to spilling your guts. Helping professionals also come with an air of privacy, which can be useful.

Tool No. 9: Books, Articles, and Videos

There are plenty of books, articles, and videos that can help you with self-reflection. When getting to know yourself, it's great to choose books with questions and exercises you can fill in. Here are some on this topic that I love:

- *What Color Is Your Parachute?*[10]
- *Business Model You.*[11]
- *The Start-Up of You.*[12]
- *How Will You Measure Your Life?*[13]

There are also some great TED Talks and articles on this subject.[14]

Tool No. 10: Balance

You might be thinking, *Balance? What does that have to do with getting to know myself better?* Well, balance is really important. If you spend all your time hacking hard on the idea of what to do next, you might actually have a pretty hard time figuring it out. It can be tempting to postpone everything else in your life until you feel as if you have this critical element deciphered, but I urge you not to. It's important to keep the other aspects of your life going, such as family, friends, home life, exercise, and extracurricular activities. Have you ever noticed how you sometimes get great ideas in the shower? These days, it's one of the only places we can be alone with our thoughts without the intrusion of distractions or cellphones, unless, of course, you have a waterproof cellphone case, which I don't advocate, since the shower is such a great place to generate ideas!

The principle is similar when it comes to non-work activities and situations — paradoxically, those times and places when we've specifically decided *not* to think about work are often when the best work-related ideas pop into our heads. They just seem to float in as if the universe had invited them there, rather than coming from your specific desire for them to arise. So if you're delaying things in life such as getting a dog, going on that date, whatever, until you get a job, I urge you not to. Going for it will prove to yourself that work isn't everything, which is an important notion, indeed. Think of the things that you love and that fill your soul — for me, that's dancing and musicals, among other things — and then do them! Being happy outside work could help you become happier at work. If you're currently in a job and you're a workaholic, try to reduce your hours. How can you come up with an idea for your next step if you don't make the time and space for it? It's important to take time away from your job so you can gain some perspective. Vacations are great for this. Taking time away can also end up making you better at what you do! You'll be more relaxed and ready to go.

I don't mean to sound like your mother, but sleep is also important. Recently, I had a conversation with someone who told me that they'd tried going from eight hours of sleep a night to seven and were struggling with it. I shared that I'd recently increased my eight to nine hours of sleep per night and was feeling extra-productive since then. Even if you "save" one hour by sleeping less, you might lose many more hours by not being productive since you're not rested enough! Sleep is like an investment with compounded returns. The more you sleep, the more energy and productivity you can have. Exercise is the same way, but too much of either can be bad. On the subject of sleep, I've heard that hitting the snooze button can actually end up making you more tired. That's an interesting fact that I thought I'd pass along, but I'm still hitting the snooze button!

One thing I make sure of, though, is to have a quiet and dark place to sleep. Believe it or not, little alarm clock lights can drastically affect the quality of your sleep. And, of course, so can sound. If your bedroom's in a noisy place (or if your partner snores), consider getting a Dohm white noise machine. People with babies buy these to help their infants sleep.

Nutrition is important, too. Eating organic, healthy meals can drastically change the way you feel about the world and yourself. And when making important decisions about your life, it's crucial to decide with the best mindset possible.

Tool No. 11: To-Do List

How is a to-do list a tool to get to know yourself? Sometimes it's easy to let your day get filled with checking the internet. But social media and email-checking is attention-seeking. Learn to get fulfillment from yourself instead and go on dates with yourself. When you wake up in the morning, the first thing you should check is yourself, not your email and the demands of others. Get out in front of your tasks and dreams and create your own to-do list so that other people's emails don't become your to-do list.

Tool No. 12: Know Thyself Questions

I've assembled a list of core questions for you to answer, a know-thyself list. Find some quiet time and a period of hours to work on them and keep coming back to the list. You can write in this book, in your journal, or both. Try to see if you can make your answers as long as possible, so you can get as much information onto the page as you can. I've listed the Know Thyself Questions here in this chapter, but you'll also find them in Appendix 3 at the end of the book with space for writing.

Know Thyself Questions

What You Love

What did you love to do when you were a child?

What do you love to do?

What extracurriculars do you participate in/love?

What are you doing when you feel the most alive? What are some activities that relax and rejuvenate you?

What topics do you love googling, reading about, learning about, or watching shows/films or listening to podcasts about?

What kinds of careers are the people you find yourself most interested in/attracted to doing?

What can you not stop thinking about?

What subjects did you love the most in school?

Who are some of the people you admire most and what do they do?

What did you like about your last job or your last few jobs? What didn't you like?

What are some of your favourite places to be? Least favourite places?

What are you most grateful for?

What do you do without being paid, just because you love it? What would you do without being paid, because you love it that much?

If you had 365 days left to live, what would you spend them doing?

What activities put you in such a state of flow that you lose track of time?

What does your ideal day look like? (Days create a week, weeks create months, months create years, and years create a lifetime. But it all starts with a day, one cycle, so if you can get that cadence down, you can change your whole life. Change your days, change your life.)

What kinds of people do you love to hang out with, or would you love to spend more time with? What are they like? What are the qualities of the types of people you'd most like to work with?

What You Can Offer

What barriers or limitations do you have?

Identify opposing/alternative thoughts/arguments to those barriers and limitations, or ways you can get around them in order to believe you have a chance of succeeding in finding a better career path for yourself.

If you didn't feel these limitations, what would your life be like? What could you offer?

We each drag luggage around with us throughout life in the form of limitations and limiting beliefs. It's helpful to leave some baggage behind. Which of the above distorted thoughts about limitations would you like to leave behind?

What's unique about you?

What are some challenges you've faced and how could you parlay the strengths and knowledge you've developed as a result of helping others, e.g. those with similar challenges?

What are your strengths?

What do your friends/peers/colleagues routinely come to you for advice on? (Leave space for people to answer these questions.)

What subjects were you best at in school?

What You Need

What are your values? (Rank them from 1 to 5. Examples: health, family, et cetera.)

To you, what is work? What's the meaning of work? What sort of value does it have? (These are questions Steve Jobs was rumoured to have asked a Buddhism teacher when he was young.)

How much money do you want and/or need to make over the course of your career? By when? What sort of annual salary do you want to command now and in the future? What will you do with that money (e.g. what will you buy)? As part of your decision, understand that after an income level of $75,000, increases in salary haven't been shown to make a material impact on happiness. As well, intrinsic goals (personal growth, feeling of community, inherent satisfaction) are much more fulfilling than extrinsic goals (money, image, status, popularity).

How You Want to Help the World

How do you wish the world could be different? What kind of culture do you want to live in?

What kind of legacy do you want to leave?

Another way you can get to the root of things is by identifying a series of "why's," e.g. if you wrote "I want to change education," you could write a follow-up question of "Why?" and answer it. Doing this five or six times will help you get past initial thoughts and go deeper, figuring out what the true essence is behind what you want to do. So, go for it. Write a few statements of how you want the world to be different or what kind of legacy you want to leave, then write five why's and answers for each.

What's the purpose of your life?

Characteristics of My Ideal Next Step

What am I looking for in a next opportunity? For this question, you could include salary, hours, time off, location, size of company, and culture (see Appendix 3). Keep in mind that we're not really considering specific titles or companies right now, just broad categories. That will come later.

PULLING IT ALL TOGETHER

In the above questions, you probably had quite long answers, which is awesome! If they weren't long, consider going back to see if you can expand on them and make them a bit longer.

In this phase, we can see if there are any patterns and pull them together into one page we can refer back to. So go through your long answers and highlight or underline patterns. Then start pulling them together into the subcategories and add them to your page. Here's an example of the output I had from this stage. These answers kept coming up again and again.

What I Love	What I Can Offer	What I Need	How I Want to Help the World	Characteristics of My Ideal Next Step
• Creating. • Performing. • Writing. • Making.	• Organizing in-person gatherings. • Writing. • Communicating. • Marketing. • Making. • Leadership.	• To be near family. • To make a good living.	• Help more people find and pursue careers that are a good fit for them. • Influence more people to choose careers that have a positive impact.	• Small team. • Flexible hours.

FIG. 5: *Pulling together my answers to Know Thyself Questions*

KNOW YOUR OPTIONS

Now what? As an output of all this, think about what careers *could* potentially go with all this newfound knowledge of yourself, e.g. what *might* you like doing. This can be big, broad categories (e.g. "something in hospitals"), rather than worrying about specific job titles or which company just yet. It's a chance to brainstorm, to think of all the wild ideas you might have, without cutting them down or thinking, "I can't do that." Why? Because you don't want to sever any possibilities. Even if you actually can't do something (e.g. can't be a horse rider due to physical limitations), write it down, anyway (in a separate section if you want), because by coming up with tons of ideas, you'll start to see themes. The more ideas, the better.

Remember that at this stage of the brainstorm you're just coming up with ideas and not culling or removing anything. That's for step 3 in the next chapter. But here, we merely come up with ideas and don't narrow them down, because you could lose out on coming up with potential possibilities when your brain is in "cut-off" mode rather than "open-up" mode. Your mind works like a parachute — it doesn't work as well when it's not open. You could think of this from an improv standpoint — the time-tested principle of saying "yes and" increases the number of possibilities, while saying "no but" decreases them. Eventually, it's important to get to "no but" (because you can't do everything), though not at first (because you need to come up with a chain of possibilities that build on one another in order to get to your best possibility). List even things you know you'd never do, in a specific area on your page that shows careers that are close to possibilities, if you wish. These might give you ideas for real possibilities.

You could also consider career possibilities to make your friends jealous, e.g. to think of the most badass thing you could do and then do it, and make sure not to do something unless it's going to make all your friends jealous. And not just your friends from your university program. A number of people in my program were jealous that I was going to be doing marketing for consumer packaged goods, but no one outside the program seemed to share the same excitement, including me, once I got out of it! Have confidence in yourself! It's not just mediocre companies that want to hire you; it's awesome ones, too! Make a list of the coolest companies you like and reach out to them (e.g. for me, that would be hot startups with awesome investors involved, Google, IDEO, et cetera). Or dream up the most amazing business you could start and apply for business plan competitions and grant programs for entrepreneurs. Think of the most interesting countries you'd like to live in. Write all these things down and draw them out. As soon as I started doing this, I began to achieve goals rapidly that I thought it would take me years to accomplish. Reach as high as you possibly can, because this is the time to do it. If you set incredibly high goals, the worst that can happen is you fall slightly short of them and *still* end up with a terrific outcome.

Here are some ways to find out about career options. Keep in mind that we're not really thinking about companies or specific titles right now, just broad categories of things:

- ☐ Google career options.
- ☐ Read.
- ☐ Call your guidance counsellor from school, or find a career counsellor.
- ☐ Talk to friends.
- ☐ Read blogs (e.g. onedayonejob.com).
- ☐ Read books such as *What Color Is Your Parachute?*
- ☐ Read recommended careers in personality tests.
- ☐ Look at job boards.
- ☐ Look at job postings on the websites of some of the companies you admire most.

You can also invent a career or think of careers you could invent, e.g. one person makes and sells board games, another runs a board game store. Wherever you can add value to people or companies and they will pay you money for it, there's a potential career. After all, in the end isn't that what careers are — adding value to other people in the world and getting remunerated for it? After all, isn't that how all careers came to be — someone first decided to do that career, or the boss gave him or her that title and then other people became it, too? There isn't some over-arching career-granting body that says, "Okay, now a new job is social media specialist. People can now become a social media specialist and companies must give people that title." Instead, it's people and companies that invent titles. To help build this list, think of popular trends right now for what careers you might potentially be a fit for or what you might like doing. Here are my examples:

What Careers Might Potentially Be a Fit (What I Might Like Doing)?

- Join a startup.
- Start a startup.
- Work at a non-profit.
- Start a non-profit.
- Venture capital.
- International development work.

FIG. 6: *Career options that might potentially fit me.*

6 Step 3: Narrowing It Down

There are some people who live in a dream world,
and there are some who face reality, and then there
are those who turn one into the other.

— DOUGLAS EVERETT

Now that you have a list of potential careers, it's time to narrow it down. This is the first cut; there will be more cuts later on. Ideally, you don't do too much cutting because you haven't had the chance to try the career yet, but there might be some obvious limitations that cause some of the career choices to be eliminated. There are some practical questions to ask. For example, "Would I need to move for that job? Am I willing to move?" Make sure at this point to differentiate between facts and assumptions. For instance, you might think you need to move to Los Angeles to be successful in the TV industry. But you might be able to stay right where you are and be successful. In one of the next steps, you'll be able to find proven ways to figure out if your assumptions are correct (e.g. by talking to five successful people in the TV industry or reading academic articles online, not by talking to your friend who auditioned for one TV show and is now working in a job he hates). But for now, just focus on facts, e.g. if the average salary for X is $30,000 and you need $40,000 annually to pay your mortgage, are you willing to give up your mortgage? Can you cut down on other expenses? Maybe you'll need to try something to decide. You can annotate your list with one of the following categories: I can't do the job, *or* I would need to change _____. And even if the average salary for a cook is lower than your budget requires, you could become the next Julia Child and earn a ton! You might come up with new ideas during this phase. No worries — add them in!

Here are some ways to cut down your list: first brainstorm and think of your hard limits, your no-go zones, or what might make a job not feasible or possible or interesting for you. Mine are: "Am I morally against this job?", "Would I have to move for this job?" (I don't want to move), "Would this job have the potential to pay me enough to live?", "Would this job allow me to have a good work/life balance?" Again, make sure you're differentiating between assumptions and facts.

CUTTING DOWN YOUR LIST

What are your hard limits or no-go zones? (For example: "I don't want to work for a company that promotes smoking.")

What might make a job not feasible, possible, or interesting for you? (For example: "I don't really know if I want to move.")

Use the above questions to cut down your career list. The table below shows you how to do this. Plot the careers across the X axis and the criteria along the Y axis. Next, assess each career's fit with each criterion, i.e., yes or no. From here, you should be able to eliminate some options. Below, you can do your own version of the table, and you can also do it in Appendix 3.

	Doctor	Dietician	Physiotherapist
Cannot make under $40,000 annually	Yes	Yes	Yes
Don't want to move	No	Yes	Yes

FIG. 7: *Cutting down my possible careers.*

Your Turn			

FIG. 7A: *Cutting down your possible careers.*

You should now be left with a list of career options that could be possible for you. You'll have crossed out ones that aren't possible because of facts and noted which ones might not be possible based on what you find out about whether the assumptions you had were right or wrong (in a next step). In my example above, I crossed out doctor and had dietician and physiotherapist remaining. Write out the options here. Recall that these categories can and should be broad, e.g. "something in hospitals." This will be a first cut, and as I said, more will be cut later. We'll also get to specific job titles later.

In Appendix 3, you can make the following lists: Careers that Could Be Possible and Careers that Could Be Possible If Assumptions Turn Out Okay.

YOUR IDEAL WORK ENVIRONMENT

Now let's move on to your ideal work environment. I'll provide a list of different attributes that a company, career, or work environment can have. These are important to consider because, for example, some people are happier in small companies while others are happier in big companies. Some people prefer to have more control while others like to receive more direction. You might want to work at a startup so you can have more autonomy. Startups are also a great way to learn a lot in a rapid manner. Or perhaps you're looking for a job that allows you to travel.

If you don't like your current job or didn't like your previous job, that might feel like a wasted opportunity. But, actually, it's not! Bad experiences can be a great opportunity to figure out what you *don't* want, and to think about what you might like instead. I used to wonder why bad and sad exist in this world, e.g. why there are wars and sicknesses. You might disagree with this view, but from my standpoint I've come to believe they exist to highlight the good in this world. If everything was good, life would just be mediocre and flat. Nothing would be happy because it would all be the same. There would be no highs or lows. So bad things and times lead us to good ones, letting us realize the brightness, beauty, and specialness of good times.

Place yourself on a scale somewhere on one end of these diametric opposites. For example:

I placed myself closer to "small company" because I want to be part of a small company. But not too small!

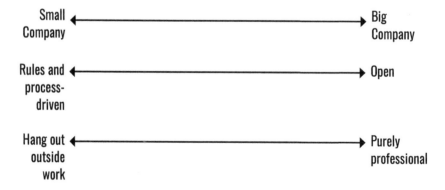

Looking at the career options through this lens will help you narrow your list further.

ONE MORE CHECK

Make sure, if you haven't already, to:

- Cross out careers that you:
  - · Can't do (practical limitations).
  - · Won't do (e.g. morally against, don't want to move, et cetera).
- Identify careers that you:
  - · Might not be able to do (assumptions).
- Cross-reference know-thyself results:
  - · Narrow options based on that (e.g. hours, pay).

You can do your list of potential career options in Appendix 3. Here's what my mine looked like at this stage:

What Careers Might Potentially Be a Fit (What I Might Like Doing)?	
· Join a startup.	· Venture capital.
· Start a startup.	· Assumption: that I could get a job in VC.
· Work at a non-profit.	· International development work.
· Start a non-profit.	· Too far from family.

FIG. 8: *My potential career options.*

Step 4: Career Design Process

Action may not always bring happiness but there is no happiness without action.

— BENJAMIN DISRAELI, *Lothair*

Now let's move from reflection to action by starting the Career Design Process. I used Stanford University's d.school design process to help develop my Career Design Process:

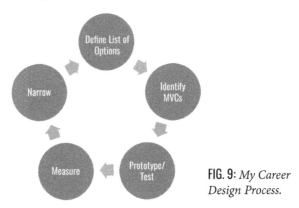

FIG. 9: *My Career Design Process.*

Now for a preview of the next six steps and chapters:

4.1. Define your list of current career options.

4.2. Identify how to learn more about the different options in the most low-commitment way possible (avoid overcommitting) using minimum viable commitment (MVC), starting with the most exciting option first.

4.3. Prototype/Test: Participate fully in trying each option. Every experience is valuable, so fail fast.

4.4. Measure: Document your experience with ratings.

4.5. Narrow: Remove options that you have, rule out others.

4.6. Repeat the cycle, deepening commitment as warranted and adding options as they come up.

8 Step 4.1: Identify Options

> The minute you realize that your options are unlimited, things just start falling into place all around you.
>
> — JOHN CUSACK

In this step, you'll want to identify your options from your last round of narrowing. Since you're starting this cycle for the first time, your options will be left over from step 3. In the chart on the next page, you can see how I identified my remaining options on the right, including the career I had an assumption about: venture capital.

For future rounds, you might have answers left over from step 4.5, "Narrow." You'll learn more about this throughout the next few chapters.

Now that you've identified your options, it's time to figure out how to try them! So we move on to the next phase: identifying minimum viable commitments (MVCs).

What Careers Might Potentially Be a Fit (What I Might Like Doing)?	Options
· Join a startup.	· Join a startup.
· Start a startup.	· Start a startup.
· Work at a non-profit.	· Work at a non-profit.
· Start a non-profit.	· Start a non-profit.
· Venture capital.	· Venture capital.
· Assumption: that I could get a job in VC.	· Assumption: that I could get a job in VC.
· International development work.	
· Too far from family.	

FIG. 10: *My remaining career options identified.*

9 Step 4.2: Minimum Viable Commitments (MVCs)

Do or do not. There is no try.

— Yoda

IDENTIFY MVCs

Now it's time to pilot the work. No, that doesn't mean you're becoming an airline pilot — unless you want to, of course! It means you're doing small trial experiences that help you figure out more about what job you want to do and what career to pursue. We'll identify how to try different career options and see if they work for you.

First, it's time to identify some potential pilot experiences. List some small ways you could try out the careers you've compiled. Do *something* — it's better to do 10 small and quick prototypes than to wait to get it perfect. You'll learn much more and get much farther than the person who just aims, aims, and aims. What we're trying to avoid here is spending eight years becoming a lawyer, without first ever seeing or understanding what a day in the life of a lawyer is like. Gaining a better understanding of what a career is *really* like will help you determine whether or not you want to invest more time in it. I call these minimum viable commitments (MVCs), the lowest commitments possible to help you get the information you need to attain the next level.

You'll rate your happiness and identify skill performance after each of the following experiences, as I'll describe in a subsequent step (4.4: "Measure"). I've placed the potential experiences on a scale ranging from less telling information, such as media browsing habits, to more telling information, such as satisfaction and performance at an internship:

- Books.
- Media browsing.
- School/college classes.
- Company videos/classes.
- Company info sessions — find out what people in your prospective careers really do. Talk to company representatives and find out what a "day in the life" is like.
- Workshops.
- Conferences/trade shows.
- Informational interviews.
- Virtual shadowing.
- In-person shadowing.
- Internships. These are important for a number of reasons. In this case, they offer a relatively short-term, risk-free opportunity to try out a career/company and see if it's right for you, if it's something you could see yourself doing in the long term.
- Jobs.

You can choose your commitments in advance or as you go along. You'll deepen them during each round. For example, here are my chosen MVCs for my career search that I did. Note how the commitment deepens for each step.

My Chosen MVCs

A. Read online articles about logistics of jobs (30 min. each).

B. Watch talks about jobs (1 hr. each).

C. Informational interviews (2 hrs. each).

D. Shadowing (1 day).

E. Shadowing (5 days).

FIG. 11: *My chosen minimum viable commitments (MVCs).*

To avoid bias, it's best if you do the same MVCs for all the career options you have.

Shadowing isn't a new idea. It's been trialled many times by many remarkable people. For example, Sean Aiken's One Week Job project saw him working at a different company every week for one year (oneweekjob.com). Maeghan Smulders launched a project in which she worked for a week at 10 different companies across North America in 112 days. I caught up with Maeghan and came to believe that this investment of time and money in herself (e.g. flights, et cetera) was more than worthwhile. In addition to amazing public relations, this project landed her a great job as director of marketing at PasswordBox. For more information about her project, check out archive.maeghansmulders.com/Home.html.

SECURE MVCs

Some of the MVCs you identify might seem difficult to secure. For instance, shadowing celebrities. So here are my top tips for securing MVCs:

- **To arrange MVCs, be bold:** The worst that can happen is that people say no. And that's not really too bad of a scenario, is it?
- **Find or guess their emails:** There are many great ways to do this on the internet. Tip: if they work at startups, chances are their email addresses are firstname@companyname.com. There are also some tools available on the internet that help you guess people's email addresses. Search the internet for the latest tools.
- **Compliment them:** People love flattery, and you're definitely more likely to get someone to take you up on your coffee invitation if it seems like an opportunity to be flattered.
- **Establish credibility/social proof:** People you've never met want to know that you're not a random killer. These days there's a lot of trust and people are way more willing to meet people off the internet, but to increase your chances of meeting with them, it's great to mention people who you know in common. This also establishes valid social proof and makes them more likely to meet with you. For example, once you've shadowed one famous person or someone they know and you mention that, it makes it easier to solidify subsequent shadow experiences.
- **Offer something of value in return:** People have offered to make free websites for me, do graphic design, et cetera, in exchange for meeting with me. If a busy and successful person has the option to meet with someone who's made an offer like that or with someone who essentially just wants to ask a series of questions, who do you think the busy person will choose?
- **You'd be surprised who's willing to meet with you:** Seriously, no one emails famous people because everyone assumes they're getting tons of emails. But if nobody emails them because they figure everyone else is doing so, then this creates an opportunity

for your email to actually get through. It can be lonely at the top, and if you treat people like human beings instead of gushing over them the way everyone else does, it will be a welcomed and refreshing experience for them.

A NOTE ON SHADOWING

You can also contact companies to set up experiences with them, such as job shadowing. I applied to and was selected as one of the top six finalists from hundreds in a competition to shadow Dave McClure, the founder of the incubator 500 Startups, for two weeks. Although I didn't end up being chosen for the shadow position, I leveraged Dave's name and my finalist title at every opportunity to secure shadow experiences. During the day, I got to work on my new job for the time being — figuring out what to do with my life. Then I got an idea: what if I emailed random strangers from the internet that I wanted to meet and asked them out for coffee? I know it's been said not to talk to strangers, but it was a decision that changed my life. I began reaching out to some of the top entrepreneurs in the world, including some of the founders of Airbnb (Joe Gebbia), Square (Randy Reddig), Kiva (Matt Flannery), and more. To my surprise, even though we'd never met, many of them said yes. Keep in mind that at this time my biography wasn't that impressive — I was unemployed except for working on a half-baked startup idea. But as I soon realized, not many people emailed them like that, so they were willing to take a chance. And there I was, sitting with these luminaries in cafés across the Bay Area.

At first I was pretty starstruck — I even asked Joe Gebbia of Airbnb if he'd really sent all those cereal boxes. But eventually I got over it and understood they were just like me. The way that happened was pretty comical. I was biking back to my co-op house in Palo Alto, and who did I see but Mark Zuckerberg. I nearly ran him over with my bike by accident. He seemed to be strolling along on one of his famous walking meetings. As he glanced over at me, a look of recognition passed over me as I thought to myself, *Holy crap, it's Mark Zuckerberg!* I bet my eyes bulged out of my head and had the effect of making me seem crazy. Plus, I inadvertently slowed down my bike a little. To my surprise, he reacted by appearing a tad, well, scared.

I was sure he'd had many experiences with fans acting weird around him. It passed through my mind that maybe I should stop and say hi or tell him something like "Hey, thanks for Facebook!" and keep on biking. Instead, I decided to respect his privacy and continued biking. As I passed, I nodded, and he nodded back slightly in return, seeming massively relieved. This experience stuck with me. I'd expected Zuckerberg to be a larger-than-life figure, somehow without negative human emotions like fear. But he was just like me. And that realization made me grasp that I could accomplish so much more than I'd previously thought.

Once I fathomed that, I began to ask the people I contacted really deep questions. I had no idea what to do with my life and didn't have much to lose. The worst that could happen was they'd decline to answer. And in all likelihood I was going to head back to Canada after all this and maybe never see them again. But once again, to my surprise, they were incredibly open and answered my tough questions. I learned why they'd chosen this path, what they didn't like about it, what they were worried about, and what they'd do if they started over. And ultimately it dawned on me that they, too, were normal people just like you and me, with hopes, fears, and dreams. And that made the idea of being an entrepreneur a lot more accessible for me.

After a while, I realized these informal coffee meetings were proving more informative than many of the classes I'd taken in university, and that I wanted to formalize this process. So I set about creating a self-education program to educate myself on the topics that I wish I'd learned more about in school, and more importantly, to help me figure out what I wanted to do next. I arranged to have shadow experiences at six different companies, an assortment of for-profits and non-profits of varying sizes, including Launchrock, Kiva, the Stanford d.school, Causes, Ashoka, and Dojo. With each of these companies, I spent one to five days learning from them but also helping them out wherever I could. At Causes, I assisted in producing success reports for clients and sat in on strategy meetings and interviews with potential hires. At Kiva, then CEO Matt Flannery let me accompany him to all his meetings for the day, like an anthropological observer.

I surrounded these experiences with volunteering at conferences, more meetings with people over coffee, living in a co-op community in Palo Alto, and auditing classes at Stanford. During this time, I learned more about the world, myself, and what I wanted to do next than I ever learned in school. I truly believe that self-education is the best path to changing yourself and the world.

At the co-op where I lived with some Stanford students and alumni, I had the opportunity to shadow and experience different lifestyle choices, ways of collaborating, and career choices. We cooked together, ate together, shared chores, and raised chickens in our backyard. It was amazing. I learned so much from them, and we even went to Burning Man together.

HOW TO SECURE A SHADOW EXPERIENCE

Here's the cold email template I used to secure meetings and shadow experiences with founders of Airbnb, Kiva, and Square. I bolded the key components for demonstration purposes only.

Subject: Dave McClure Shadow Finalist

Dear Stew,
I don't normally cold email celebrities, but in this case I felt compelled to do so — **I really admire your work** with Mint. **I am a** young entrepreneur who is also from Canada and recently quit my job @ P&G, packed up my life, and moved down to SF — I am also one of the top 6 finalists out of a few hundred applicants to shadow Dave McClure for 2 weeks. I'm at the very early stages of my new startup — a calendar service that lets you see when your friends are free or busy using any calendar system

on any device. I know you are probably very busy, but I was wondering if I could possibly grab **5 minutes of your time** over the next few days to **just learn from you**, perhaps over coffee.

Hope to hear from you soon,
Jenn

Here are some other recommendations on how to secure a shadow experience. If you want to meet speakers at conferences, the best way is to approach them after their talks. It's an easy way to find them and they're generally in the mood to answer questions afterward. Following up after a conference is always a good idea and you can establish credibility by saying: (1) "I love what you're doing," (2) "How can I help?", and (3) "You can learn more about me via my portfolio" (and make sure you have a good portfolio!).

When establishing connections, it's great to offer help in an attempt to create more value than you capture. Another idea is to make meeting with you so attractive that they end up asking you to meet up. A way to do that is to treat people, regardless of their stature, like equals rather than as if they're better than you. Most famous people just want to be treated normally, not fawned over, because that can be awkward. So approaching them as an equal can be quite refreshing to them. Think about it: if you were them, would you rather hang out with someone who acts deferent to you or someone who seems like an equal? Unless they're looking for a big ego trip, they probably want to hang out with people who feel like equals. Someone who I have a lot of respect for and who I see as further along in business than me changed the game for me when he said, "I'm not your mentor. We're peers. We can both learn things from each other." He pointed out that it's not all about who's made the most money. Even if someone has more money than the person they're talking to, they might be seeking advice in other areas such as romance, friendships, et cetera.

It's great to provide value to such people as much as possible. Here's an example of how that worked for me. A while ago my personal website left a lot to be desired. A student at my alma mater emailed me and asked if she could create a new website for me for free and link it to her portfolio on the slick website she'd made for herself. Of course, I said yes! Only after we began working together did she start asking me a few small mentorship questions and request some minor introductions. That was a great way to get her foot in the door with me!

As much as I'd like to say I'm not selfish, I am busy. So when I get a request from someone along the lines of "Hey, can I come ask you questions about your life for a few hours?" I'm ashamed to admit that the answer is often no. I plan to change that in the future and offer more of my time once I'm farther along the startup path, but for now I'm pretty busy grinding it out and thus trying to kill birds with one stone by packaging a lot of my advice into this book. But for now, the inquiries that are easiest to say yes to are those that offer value in return, whether it be photos of my office, a free promo video, writing a blog post about my experience, being a prospective employee, and so on. There are things that might not take too much work on behalf of the party offering it to me, but the benefits could be invaluable. You never know the effect you might have on someone. I suspect that a lot of people sort through things in a similar way to me and realize now that I probably could have gotten more yeses to my shadow proposal if I'd offered something in return. In the end, the young lady who designed my website has received a number of things from me, including a testimonial, a reference letter, and hours of free advice (for what it's worth) by telephone.

A word of caution about email etiquette: stick to double-blind introductions. What's a double-blind introduction? Well, have you ever been cc'd on an email introducing you to someone without your permission? I *hate* that. I wasn't necessarily looking to meet that person, but now I feel obligated to because *you* introduced us. A double-blind introduction is the opposite of that. Instead of randomly cc'ing people together who you think might get along and then hitting send, you approach the parties and ask them individually if they might like to be introduced to so-and-so and then provide some biographical details about so-and-so. Unless they both say yes, don't introduce them!

Think of the most badass people you can imagine. Send them an email. What's the worst that can happen? What have you got to lose? Or put another way, what might you potentially lose out on if you opt *not* to get in touch with them? I'd argue that it's a bigger risk not to get in touch with them than it is to do so. It's not as if they're going to email you and ask, "Who do you think you are?" and then post something negative about you on social media. Probably the worst that could happen is they hit Archive or Delete on your message and you never hear from them. Well, guess what, there's nothing to stop you from emailing back in a few years — except perhaps a few well-placed spam filters, if they're really diligent — and trying again.

TAKE A TRIP

You might be thinking to yourself, *How can I get a shadow experience with someone when no one in my town is doing <insert desired career options here>*. Or perhaps you're flooded with opinions from those around you about going into the "hot companies" in your city, but you're not sure if you should try something elsewhere. Even if you do your hardest not to listen to the job gossip going on around you, it's difficult not to let it creep up on you. My solution for this is to get out of the bubble. If you can scrape together the money to do it, or if you can find a company that will fly you somewhere for an interview, I strongly suggest booking a trip of at least a weekend, or more ideally a week, to somewhere relevant to what you want to do, either a country you badly want to work in or the "hub" location for the field you're into. In other words, if you're interested in technology/entrepreneurship, go to Silicon Valley. If it's advertising/finance, head to New York City. For music/movies, jet to Los Angeles. Trust me, the time and money are worth it.

There's one important thing to do beyond booking the flights, though. In advance of your trip, do research to figure out who you think is doing the coolest stuff there, then email them to set up meetings for when you arrive. Learn from them about the scene, their companies, and what advice they have. Bonus points if you find someone who's doing what you'd like to be involved with a few years from now. When I first visited Silicon Valley, I found and reached out to everyone from angel investors to founders of Square and Airbnb. People are surprisingly accessible and willing to meet with you, especially when you're nice and if you try to provide value to them.

As places to visit go, I highly recommend Silicon Valley. Here's an example of how crazy awesome it can be. One day, when I was in San Francisco, I went to work at a coffee shop, and who ended up sitting across from me but Tim Ferriss! In case you haven't heard of him, he's the author of *The 4-Hour Workweek*, a book I've read multiple times and that has definitely helped inspire me on my journey![1] Beside me was a girl doing a terrific adventure of her own, completing a bunch of her dreams in 60 days (iris60days.com). When I mentioned that I thought it might be Tim Ferriss sitting across from us, she said her journey was actually somewhat inspired by him, as well, and asked me to film an interview of her with him. I also got a video of Tim talking about my startup at the time! How crazy is that?

10 Step 4.3: Prototype/Test

Living on the edge is totally scary, however, it's the only place that has the best view.

— SEAN STEPHENSON

It's time to take action on your MVCs. Now that you've set them up, approach them with the most vigour you can. It's easy to let an MVC experience be coloured by judgment, self-doubt, or worry — or what I call "futurizing" (thinking too much about what the future holds without being present enough to take in the current moment). There are a few ways you can combat this to get the most out of your MVCs:

1. **Find ways to test your assumptions and track these results:**
   When you're preparing for an MVC experience, think about what assumptions you might be able to verify or nullify through it. For example, maybe you're concerned that advertising might be too cutthroat and you're about to meet with an advertising executive. Ask the person about it — ideally, in as non-judgmental a way

as possible. This is a great opportunity to acquire information to help you understand if your assumptions are true or false. Keep in mind that there might be some bias involved — people are inherently more likely to say positive things about their career choices than negative things as a way of justifying, if even only just to themselves, that the decisions they made were good ones. So it's helpful to ask your key questions to multiple people in the field if possible and to back them up with research about related studies before deciding if something is "true" or not. After your experience, you could track your results regarding your assumptions as follows:

Option	Assumptions	Results
Venture capital	That I could get a job in venture capital	Correct — venture capitalist said so during informational interview

FIG. 12: *Options, assumptions, and results.*

2. **Suspend judgment, worry, or doubt:** You might be tempted to hold back, to be too in your head about things, and to be constantly analyzing whether this feels like the right thing for you. Believe it or not, that's exactly the *opposite* of what you should do. My recommendation is that you immerse yourself fully in the experience and suspend judgment until *after* you've completed the experience. That way you can get as close as you can to experiencing "a day in the life" and then when you get home you can analyze how the experience fits with the criteria you set out for what your best career and life could look like. In many

experiences, you're simultaneously in two modes: *being* and *judging*. In *being*, you're in the moment, you're doing what's in front of you. In *judging*, you're analyzing whether what's in front of you is the right thing to do. As part of this book, we're working toward getting you into a career where you spend a larger portion of your time *being* rather than *judging*. But in these early stages of career exploration, you'll be naturally inclined to focus more on *judging* than *being*. This is problematic for a number of reasons, most notably that allocating brain resources to *judging* can take away from *being*, which creates a cycle in which you essentially end up judging your judging! Far more effective is to plunge yourself fully into an experience once you've decided to do it. Later on, once you've selected a career and have been steeped in it for a few years, if you suddenly discover you're spending much more time *judging* than *being*, that might be a sign to consider what your next career change should be. But for now, while you're in the career-choosing process, you've picked these MVCs, and by virtue of that, you've committed to them. Don't worry about whether this is the right thing to try right now, or if there's something else you've missed, or if you're good at it. There's plenty of time to think about those things later and to improve on each of these dimensions. Someone said something powerful to me recently: "If you don't know what to do, think of what you would do if you did know what to do." Apply this to whatever chosen MVC experience you've selected and then have at it! If it's a shadow experience, be the best shadow you can. If it's an informational interview, ask questions to the extreme! Just be sure you *participate fully*.

3. **Participate fully:** How do you get out of your head and immerse yourself fully in the experience? You do it by focusing on participation. It's been said that if there's a thought in your head that you don't want to think about, it's not very effective to try to get rid of it by musing to yourself, *Don't think about that*. Let me show you by example. Say I asked you not to think about a purple rhinoceros. What are you thinking about now? How about now? Instead of

trying to *force* a thought out of your head by sheer willpower, try *replacing* it with something. For me, what helps to be present is to focus intensely on the details of the scenario in front of me. I look at the furniture around me, I listen to the tone of people's voices and I pay attention to what people say. In acting, this is called the Meisner technique. My understanding of the Meisner technique is that actors are directed to focus on their fellow actors and what they're doing instead of concentrating on themselves and their own anxieties and trying to remember their lines. When actors do this, they end up responding more naturally and giving better performances! It's a remarkable way for people to become more confident in social situations. Somewhat counterintuitively, spending all their time deeply listening to their conversation partner helps them come up with or recall better and more natural responses than if they'd devoted the time to think of a response. And it's a great way to become more present and focus more on *being* rather than *judging*. If you're shadowing, ask how you can help out. If you're doing an informational interview, concentrate intensely on the features of the person's face, without seeming creepy, of course!

4. **Be prepared to rate your feelings and performance afterward:** Now that you've participated fully and finished an MVC experience, it's time to immediately rate your experience. Make sure to do this right after each and every experience. If you've waited until you've gone through all the different experiences, you've waited too long — it'll be too hard to remember how each of the experiences were on their own and you'll just be comparing distant memories. You'll evaluate the experiences together later, but for now it's good to focus on each of them on their own. You might thinking, *What's with all this specificity and science?* The reason from my standpoint is that we're trying to apply a semi-scientific decision-making process to our career selection. That way we can hopefully make a better choice than if we just flip a coin. In effect, we're throwing spaghetti at a wall to see what sticks. I'll explain more about how to measure your experiences in the next step and chapter.

Step 4.4: Measure

> You're in competition with one person only: the individual you know you can become.
>
> — Martha Graham

In this step, you'll reflect on your small pilot of each career option and keep notes on how you enjoyed them, how good you were at them, and how the careers seem to align (or not align) with the criteria you set out earlier.

On the following page is an example of how I rated my experience of reading articles about launching a startup. This was the first MVC level I decided to try with each of my different career options I was choosing from. I haven't filled the rest out, but you get the idea.

As you can see, I listed how long I spent on the option, how I liked it, how good I was at it, how well it matched my needs, and how it seemed to help the world. Then I scored the option at that point, out of 40, with 10 points allocated to each of the categories.

A. Define List of Options	Join a Startup	Start a Startup	Work at a Non-Profit	Start a Non-Profit	Venture Capital
B. Identify MVCs	Read articles online and read logistical information about each role (e.g. salary, career path, et cetera).				
C. Prototype/test	30 min.	2 hrs.	40 min.	30 min.	50 min.
D. Measure How I liked it		10/10. Enjoyed reading.			
How good I was at it		9/10. I paid attention and read for a long time.			
How it fits with my needs		10/10. Fit my needs for independence.			
How it might help the world					
Discoveries re assumptions					
E. Narrow (continue?)	Y	39/40	24/40 — N	Y	Y

FIG. 13: *My round 1 list of minimum viable commitments.*

12 Step 4.5: Narrow

The reasonable man adapts himself to the world; the unreasonable man persists in trying to adapt the world to himself. Therefore all progress depends on the unreasonable man.

— George Bernard Shaw,
Man and Superman

Now that you've rated your experience for MVC round 1, it's time to narrow for MVC round 2. You can start by tallying the scores and putting them into a chart like the one on the next page.

If at any step in the process you identify that one of the options falls below a certain threshold of criteria for you, you might decide you no longer wish to continue pursuing MVCs for that option. In this table, I provide an example of how I realized working at a non-profit wasn't a fit for me after reading articles about it. If you run into something like that, you might decide not to deepen your commitment for

MVC/Option	Join a Startup	Start a Startup	Work at a Non-Profit	Start a Non-Profit	Venture Capital	Author
A. Read online articles about logistics of jobs (30 min. each)	35	39	25 — N	35	30	—
B. Watch talks about jobs (1 hr. each)	32	38	—	31	31	—
C. Informational interviews (2 hrs. each)	35	37	—	30	28	—
D. Shadowing (1 day)	31	31	—	30	20 — N	32

Tally scores at end of each round. Not all rounds eliminate options. New options can be added anytime.

FIG. 14: *My round 2 list of minimum viable commitments.*

that option, e.g. you could choose not to proceed with your other MVCs (in my case, watching talks, doing an informational interview, shadowing, et cetera). This is the narrowing phase.

The first large circle displays how not all rounds of MVCs will eliminate options. Some options might persist throughout all the rounds, and that's completely fine. So you don't always need to narrow.

The small circle on the right shows how new options can be added anytime. As you're going through this process, I encourage you to keep casting a net. If you find something of interest that wasn't on your initial list, add it and go through the steps for it. In this case, I realized that being an author was of interest to me once I was at the shadowing stage for all of my other options. So I added it! With new options, you can start at the beginning of the MVC levels with them and progress through each level from the start — or jump right into the middle of the levels. So in my case I could have started at level 1 with reading articles about being an author, or begun at any other MVC level. I chose to jump right in with an experience of shadowing an author.

13 Step 4.6: Repeat

There's more to life than the everyday routine, keep this in mind until Life becomes your dream.

— BERNHARD FLEISCHMANN

Before proceeding to the next MVC level, evaluate the last round to see if you want to add or eliminate any options in the narrowing step. Now it's time to deepen your commitment to each option by proceeding to the next MVC level. In the table in the previous chapter, I moved from my MVC level 1 of reading online articles to MVC level 2 of watching talks, but I excluded the option of the non-profit job because I'd already eliminated it in the narrowing stage.

This step is all about rating your options to choose the top careers from that list, then deepening the commitment by selecting another pilot opportunity for each career. You'll continue repeating steps 4.1 to 4.5 until you've narrowed down to your top three options. In my case, as you can see on the following page, my top three options ended up being joining a startup, starting a startup, and being an author:

MVC/Option	Join a Startup	Start a Startup	Work at a Non-Profit	Start a Non-Profit	Venture Capital	Author
D. Shadowing (1 day)	31	31	—	30	20 — N	32
E. Shadowing (5 Days)	(36)	(39)	—	21 — N	—	(33)

FIG. 15: *My top three career options.*

Keep trying things until you've narrowed down your list to three or so careers you really think you might like, be good at, make money from, and that might help the world. Here's another example of what your table could end up looking like:

Event/Measures	Physiotherapist	Dietician
My pilot experience	Physiotherapists' Conference	Informational interview
How I liked it	9 out of 10	6 out of 10
How good I was at it	7 out of 10	N/A
How much I would make	Found out average salary was $80,000	Average salary $40,000
Would it help the world?	Yes — healing people	Yes
Location	Don't need to move	Don't need to move
Conclusion	Want to learn more	Crossing off my list

FIG. 16: *Example list of careers narrowed down.*

In the above table, I crossed dietician off the list and still had physiotherapist to investigate. What are you crossing off your list? Instead of having to predict what jobs you think you might like, this method gives you real data and a scoring system to show you the careers you'd be happiest in. Make a table similar to mine above and start identifying pilot experiences, trying them, and then tracking the results.

If the options you're left with are too broad to be actionable, e.g. "Start a startup," "What kind of startup?", et cetera, repeat the steps to develop new and more specific options to narrow it down, e.g. to "start a maker-space for kids, a maker kit company for kids, or an online maker learning platform for kids."

You can also repeat this process as necessary for other aspects of your choices, e.g. if you determine you want to join a startup, you could identify potential companies and run the process again to narrow them down.

14 Your Top Three

Risk more than others think is safe. Care more than others think is wise. Dream more than others think is practical. Expect more than others think is possible.

— CLAUDE BISSELL

Now create a list of your top three career choices. Keep in mind that these can change in the future. We're not creating a list of our perfect careers for life — in fact, I don't believe there is such a thing. We're creating a list of our top three career choices for *now*. They might change in the future. In fact, with people changing careers an average of nine times in their lifetimes, it might be rare if you didn't change careers a couple of times before you die!

If you're really having trouble narrowing your potential careers, here's a trick I like. It seems simplistic, but it can be effective. Picture yourself in each of the chosen careers. Try to envision what your typical day will look like. Do you like that day? If you really can't decide, you can even flip a coin to help narrow your choices. But to make the decision better than random chance, if you don't like the side of the coin that turned face up, perhaps the other option was the better one for you.

At some point you need to choose; otherwise, you'll get stuck in analysis paralysis. And though it will feel as if you've avoided making a decision, that actually won't be the case. You'll have made a decision *not* to decide. That's inherently a choice to stick with the status quo and not take a risk on something that might make you happier. Looking back, will you be more pleased with staying stagnant or taking a risk? Even if it doesn't work out, taking the risk is probably the better choice because if you don't, you'll never know what might have happened. And my best guess is that your next career step *will* work out, especially since you've put so much work into it (assuming you've done all the exercises in this book so far).

Write down your top three career choices (in no particular order) here:

1. _____

2. _____

3. _____

Now, for each job make a plan, including your analysis, vision, course of action, and associated income. Write out your assumptions. Act on your plan and then record a cost/benefit analysis, then review, revise, and repeat. That's how we grow.

To perform a cost/benefit analysis, analyze (you guessed it!) the costs and benefits of particular courses of action. What's the potential benefit out of 10? The potential risk? If the spread is big enough (e.g. potential risk level of 2 versus a potential benefit level of 8), choose to take the action. For example, if I wanted to select whether or not to franchise a business, I might think about the fact that the risk of doing so is fairly low — it could fail, I could lose a couple of thousand dollars, I could end up in some verbal disagreements, or I could become embroiled in a legal battle, or more than one. But these are all solvable issues. I'd rate this as a risk level of 2 in the overall grand scheme of things. But the benefit of franchising could be immense. I could end up selling tons of franchises and offering my concept to millions of kids around the world. I'd rate this as a benefit level of 8, or even higher. So I choose to franchise. What is worth the risk for you?

When you're making your decisions, consider whether you're doing them from a place of love and peace or a place of fear and unhappiness. If it's the latter, think again. Before settling on a big decision, it's ideal to get yourself into a good mindset, whether it's through dancing, reading, or waiting until another day.

Please note that you don't need to choose only one career. Some people have what are called "portfolio careers," which consists of many different commitments in a given day, month, or year. People's attention has changed, and gone are the days when we picked one career and stuck with it for our whole lives. Here's a side note: did you know that in Japan it's actually illegal to fire people?

Those of us who have the ability to change careers can consider ourselves lucky. Monogamy is becoming less prevalent and polyamory — having multiple loves — is moving in. People are transitioning from being "serial monogamists," where they're with only one person at a time and they keep on switching who they're with one after the other, to dating multiple people at a time. The same goes for careers: for some people, having to pick only one career can feel limiting. And with so many hours in the week, who's to say that having only one career is necessary? Some say to focus on only one thing and then you'll be better at it. Paul Graham, the co-founder of Y Combinator, says in one of his essays, "The Top Idea in Your Mind," something along the lines of only being able to have one thing that you think about in the shower.[1] And that's a good point. Some people do best if they only focus on one thing at a time. But others, remarkably, can be more productive if they concentrate on multiple things at once, drawing energy from many different activities in order to fuel the others. So you can become a poly-careerist, shall we say, or have a poly-career.

Plus, work spans are shortening. On average, people have around seven career changes in their lives. If you think of a total career timespan as an average of 45 years (e.g. ages 20 to 65), or even 50 years (e.g. ages 15 to 65), that means staying in a career for around six to seven years. If you think about it, that isn't long. It's certainly different from the careers of yesteryear that saw people working at the same company for 30-plus years straight. It's my belief that people will end up having even more career changes in this lifetime, especially with retirement age increasing beyond 65.

15 Closing the Deal

Our deepest fear is not that we are inadequate. Our deepest fear is that we are powerful beyond measure. It is our light, not our darkness that most frightens us. We ask ourselves, Who am I to be brilliant, gorgeous, talented, fabulous? Actually, who are you not to be? You are a child of God. Your playing small does not serve the world. There is nothing enlightened about shrinking so that other people won't feel insecure around you. We are all meant to shine, as children do. We were born to make manifest the glory of God that is within us. It's not just in some of us; it's in everyone. And as we let our own light shine, we unconsciously give other people permission to do the same. As we are liberated from our own fear, our presence automatically liberates others.

— MARIANNE WILLIAMSON, *A Return to Love*[1]

This chapter is all about closing the deal — getting an awesome company to extend you an offer. Or ideally, getting multiple offers from different companies! Instead of doing this as the first step, we're doing it as the last step of our process — for many reasons, such as being able to have a great and genuine answer when asked the inevitable question: "Why do you want to work here?" One of the many benefits of narrowing before applying is that you can take the time to send in an amazing application and wow them, leading to you having a much better chance of landing the role, rather than sending out tons of mediocre applications that are unlikely to receive replies. Here are the steps:

1. **Identify what's necessary to be a successful candidate for each of your top three choices:** Use the information you gained during prototyping, then prototype more as necessary in order to figure out what you need to succeed. You can ascertain this by asking existing employees, doing research online, reviewing job descriptions, and so on. You might find that you're able to adapt and position your background in a way that makes you the perfect candidate! Or you might find that you need to do some more work to achieve this. But that's no big deal — it's possible!

2. **Make yourself the best candidate:** Build your portfolio. Teach yourself the skills you need. Find executive education opportunities. There are many examples, e.g. online coding classes, books about do-it-yourself electronics, et cetera. There are lots of opportunities for executive education, such as the Singularity University program at NASA. People there learn about technologies like 3D printing and robotics and how to apply them to areas such as health and education. Singularity changes its curriculum every year. It also has five-day executive education programs.

    You might find that you don't need to go to graduate school to specialize in something or get a job in it. These days, portfolios really matter. It's more about what you've *done* than what you've studied. So, if you notice that your perfect job requires having a background in marketing but you don't have one, get one! It might not take as long as you think to do this.

Here are my steps to become an expert in anything, using the example of wanting to cultivate a background in marketing:

- **Find out who the existing experts are:** Google your chosen topic — marketing in this case — and find out who everyone is linking to, whose YouTube videos are most popular, and whose books rank highest on Amazon. These methods can help you figure out who the current experts are on a given topic. They might not tell you who the best academics on the subject are, but they'll reveal whose popular opinions are being listened to, and that counts. For example, I deem digital entrepreneur Neil Patel to be an expert on marketing, since whenever I Google the subject, he comes up.
- **Consume the experts' material:** Whether it's a book, a webinar, or a YouTube video, get to know what the experts are saying. For instance, I've read many of Neil Patel's articles, watched his webinars, and even enrolled in his online course.
- **Determine what it takes to succeed:** After consuming the experts' materials, distill what it takes to succeed in marketing into a few key steps.
- **Succeed:** Based on your new-found knowledge, find a way to do a project that demonstrates your skills. In the case of marketing, you could find a friend with a business and offer to market it for free. Or maybe you have an idea of your own you might like to promote. Build a full-on campaign and get results. This is a great way to demonstrate your proficiency in marketing, even though you just gained it!
- **If you don't succeed, try and try again:** This is self-explanatory. If your first marketing campaign is a flop, learn some more and try again. Employers might not want to employ someone who comes to

them with failed experiences. Ideally, you can show some results.

- **Package your success:** Find a way to communicate your success to your prospective employer. For example, you could put your project on your résumé, make an infographic (or hire someone at Fiverr to do so) that indicates the great results of your campaign, or create a website or a page on your portfolio that shows the graphics you made, media you secured, and results the campaign garnered. This is how you go from zero to hero in an area! You can also do things like meet the experts (via the cold emailing method). So you don't necessarily have to attend school to become an expert in marketing. This is becoming more and more acceptable these days. School is only one part of the picture.

Here are further steps — more on this in subsequent chapters:

3. **Apply:** Send applications that wow them.
4. **Accept the best offer — for you:** Don't just judge offers based on money. Judge them based on all the criteria you've assembled.
5. **Repeat this process as necessary:** If you want a change, or if new opportunities come up, begin the process again to find a new next career step!

Now let's look at how to land that job.

16 Land the Job

A man who truly wants to make the world better
should start by improving himself and his attitudes.

— FRED DeARMOND

FIND THE JOB: THE SPRAY-AND-PRAY APPROACH

Use Indeed to find job listings, but recognize that 80 percent of employment positions never get posted. So understand that it's also about who you know. You can improve that metric by meeting more people and conducting informational interviews. Don't ask directly if they're hiring. Instead, impress them. Perhaps they'll ask you if you're looking for a position.

A wise university program director once told me that the process of landing an interview is akin to selling a product because a similar sales cycle is involved. The more applications you send out, the more interviews you'll get. The more interviews you do, the more secondary interviews you'll get. The end result? The more secondary interviews you land, the more job offers you'll receive! Having your pick of job offers gives you more of a chance to get a job you want. The interview process will help you decide which company you're most interested in working for, as you learn more about them through interviews.

You might find that some job postings that appeal to you require more qualifications than you have. My advice? Apply for them, anyway. If you wow someone enough with your knowledge of search engine optimization (SEO) and the latest marketing techniques, they may not care that you don't have an M.B.A. It's all about what you can do for the company. With good options out there, why not apply for the very best jobs you can find? Even if you think you're underqualified, it doesn't necessarily make sense for *you* to be the one to decide that. You might be selling yourself short and making the decision before you've even stepped up to the plate to bat. That being said, I'm not advocating to apply for jobs you're wildly underqualified for. In the next chapter, we look at how you can make your experience impressive enough that nearly anyone will want to hire you. But for now it makes sense to select the very best job options you want to apply for.

One of my friends who runs a large franchised company told me that some of the best hires at his head office have been people who were working at bars or in retail. Now they're running the operations of this multi-million-dollar company. My friend said that what he looks for is a growth mindset, the belief and ability to teach oneself anything and then execute it. This is the opposite of a fixed mindset, or the belief that one's personality and skills are fixed or "born that way" and aren't malleable. With this attitude, it becomes very difficult to learn new skills or take on new roles. To learn more about growth mindset, google psychologist Carol Dweck.[1] If given a choice between hiring based on skills or personality, e.g. if I can't find someone who has both, I would always hire someone with an awesome personality, because you can always teach skills, but you can't teach awesome! Many of my entrepreneurial friends agree with that sentiment. So be awesome! And bring examples of how you have a growth mindset, e.g. examples that show how you've taught yourself something in order to build something great. For instance, maybe you taught yourself about the leading social media practices to help run social media marketing at your previous employer, which led to an increase in sales there. Or maybe you wanted to learn a new language, so you bought books, downloaded audiobooks, and found a conversation partner. Results are key to display, as well — what sort of percentage revenue increase did you help drive? How fast did you learn the language and in what contexts were you able to use it?

Now that you've found a few job opportunities that sound exactly like what you want, let's focus on what you can do to be chosen for the job. In the next chapters, I detail the ideas I've learned on how to land a job, but things change over time and vary with different disciplines, so you should go to workshops at your university, college, or career centre to learn more about these subjects. I'm a big fan of workshops!

17 Your Résumé

It is one of the most beautiful compensations of this life, that no man can sincerely try to help another without helping himself.

— RALPH WALDO EMERSON

I use a special formula for optimizing my résumé, and 99 percent of the people who have followed it have successfully obtained the job choices they applied for. It's all about portraying your experiences in the best possible light using action words and impeccable formatting. You need to have a résumé that stands out and is selected out of a pile of hundreds. Make sure to explain your experience rather than merely listing it and to tailor your résumé to each opportunity. Use salient points, e.g. raised $42,000, rather than generalities, e.g. "created PowerPoints." Here's my format:

JENNIFER TURLIUK

Phone: 647-555-5555 Email: name@website.com
Portfolio: http://www.jenniferturliuk.com
LinkedIn: http://linkedin.com/in/jenniferturliuk

SUMMARY OF QUALIFICATIONS:

- Entrepreneurial leader with a strong background in strategy, marketing, business development, and writing.
- Work featured in *New York Times*, *Wired*, *Fast Company*, *Forbes*, Harvard case study, and more.
- Training from Procter & Gamble, Singularity University at NASA, and business school at Queen's University.
- Qualified to work in Canada and U.S.A. (hold O-1 Visa: "Individual with Extraordinary Ability/Achievement").

EXPERIENCE:

MakerKids — CEO (2015–Present; Co-President (2014–2015); Co-Executive Director (2013–2014); Makerspace Coordinator (2013)

- Grew revenue 4,600%, hired and led team, secured clients (Intel, Toronto Public Library, etc.) and developed curriculum for them, delivered maker education (e.g. 3D printing, robotics) to thousands of kids/educators.

Koru Labs Inc — Founder and CEO (2011–2013)

- Secured clients and provided PR, marketing, writing, sales, and strategy services. Secured press in *Fast Company*, *Huffington Post*, *Wired*, *New York Times*, etc. Boosted 3D scanner crowdfunding campaign by three times.
- Selected for Start-Up Chile: received $40,000 in funding and supported entrepreneurship in Chile for eight months.

Procter & Gamble — Assistant Brand Manager (2010–2011), Shopper Marketing (2008)

- Commercial leader on P&G's largest brand: led strategy, multi-functional team, and agencies. In charge of Tide Pods launch (biggest launch in 27 years) and digital strategy for P&G Fabric Care brands.

Queen's University Marketing and Communications — Special Projects Assistant (2007–2009), Marketing Assistant (2007)
- Project manager for university's in-house advertising agency, interfacing between clients and designers to produce publications and more. Developed university's social media strategy, wrote copy, created contests.

EDUCATION:

Singularity University Graduate Studies Program at NASA Ames
- Selected as one of 80 students from 3,000 applicants and awarded scholarship. Won Android App Challenge.

Bachelor of Commerce (Honours), Queen's University
- Completed independent study and published paper with Ken Wong (Canadian Marketing Hall of Fame).
- Ran the Queen's Entrepreneurs' Competition, the largest international undergraduate business plan competition in Canada. Led 16-member team, raised sponsorship, developed partnership with TV show.

AWARDS AND RECOGNITION:

- Jury Captain for Core77 Design Awards, Blue Ribbons at Maker Faires, Duke of Edinburgh Awards from Prince Edward, Singularity University scholarship, Start-Up Chile, university scholarships, O-1 visa.

PUBLICATIONS:

- *Forbes* — "How I Figured Out What to Do with My Life" (900,000 views, on *Forbes* Most Read list).
- *MAKE* — "7 Cornerstones of Making with Kids" (print edition), online articles.
- *Strategy* — "Future-Transforming Ideas: Inroads into Fashion."
- *Venturebeat* — "Inside Singularity University."

TALKS: MakerCon Europe (keynote speaker), MakerCon New York, Maker Faire Bay Area, TEDxSantiago (in Spanish).

LANGUAGES: English (native), Spanish (intermediate), French (beginner).

HOBBIES: Kiteboarding, writing, dancing, yoga, DJing, self-education, entrepreneurship programs.

18 Your Cover Letter

Many a false step was made by standing still.

— FORTUNE COOKIE

Simply put, you must send a cover letter. I discard any job applications to my company that don't have one. To me, no cover letter says you don't have time to put in the effort to send a full application to my company. So why should I take the time and effort to interview you?

For your cover letter, it's important to tailor your paragraphs to skills that the company is looking for. Here's my sample cover letter from a few years ago:

Jennifer Turliuk
123 Fake St.
Kingston, ON K7L 3R1
January 19, 2007

Dear [Insert name of recruiter here],

I am excited to submit my application for the position of Assistant Brand Manager at Procter & Gamble. After learning more about the company at an info session, I realized that I wanted to pursue a career with P&G because its values match my passions for marketing, CSR, and personal development. As a Bachelor of Commerce graduate from Queen's University, I know that I am an excellent candidate due to my strong track record of leadership skills, marketing experience and academic achievement.

My leadership skills are evident in my organization of the Queen's Entrepreneurs' Competition for the past three years, most recently as the Co-Chair. I personally secured $42,070 of sponsorship, repeated in-kind media sponsorship from the *National Post*, a partnership with CBC's *Dragon's Den* TV show, a "dragon" from the show named Brett Wilson as a keynote speaker, and 30 entrepreneurial judges, including the founder of Air Miles and the CEO of UBS. To promote charity and volunteerism among my peers, I organized fundraisers and group volunteer trips as the Co-Chair of Queen's Commerce Outreach, now called Students in Free Enterprise. I also held other volunteer positions such as salsa dancing instructor, orientation leader for First Years Not in Residence, mentor to younger students, floor representative, tour guide, and radio host. At P&G, my ability to motivate and lead others will lead to success in my role.

I gained practical marketing experience this summer at the Department of Marketing and Communications at Queen's University. I developed concepts for publications as a project manager and took the initiative to create a Marketing Process document and a Student Life Video Contest. My understanding of advertising and marketing will help me to execute breakthrough marketing campaigns as an Assistant Brand Manager.

My academic achievement is demonstrated through the numerous awards and scholarships I received during my education. I consistently excelled in my classes, added value by being an active participant, and was known by each of my professors. Last year I secured an independent study course with the top marketing professor at Queen's. My motivation and dedication to learning coupled with my ability to think critically and creatively about the world will allow me to quickly analyze multiple sources of data and come to actionable conclusions in a position with P&G.

I know that I am the best candidate for the ABM position at P&G because of my leadership ability, marketing expertise, and history of academic excellence. I would love the opportunity to speak with you over the phone soon about this opportunity and can be reached at [phone number]. Thank you for reviewing my application.

Sincerely,
Jennifer Turliuk

As part of the cover letter idea, let's consider what else might attract employers' attention — the "spice." I've had people write lesson plans, develop graphics, send snail mail, make videos, and more to accompany their job applications. Sounds like a lot of work? You bet, but guess whose résumés made it to the top of the pile immediately? I know someone who launched a campaign on why Google should hire him and it went viral. He got a job interview from Google (having not received one from his previous applications there), but he didn't get the job. He did, however, get an awesome marketing position elsewhere! Check out his campaign by googling "Google Please Hire Me" — his YouTube video alone garnered 1.5 million views, and he received massive press coverage for this project. What kind of campaign can you create that's in line with your target employer's goals and values? How can you demonstrate how awesome you are? Make sure not to be creepy, and make certain your efforts show off your job-relevant skills, e.g. sending baked goods might make it look as though you're trying too hard, and they might go bad on the way.

19 Your Online Brand

Empty pockets never held anyone back. Only empty heads and empty hearts can do that.

— Norman Vincent Peale

If you want a job, clean up your online profile in case anyone still manages to get onto it (e.g. through other people's profiles, accounts, et cetera). My graduating class's accounting professor drove home the ultimate lesson in the importance of this at one of our graduation events. He got access to our Facebook profiles through another professor many of us had "friended" and proceeded to display the most embarrassing pictures of us possible on the big screen for all of our classmates and business school staff members to see. In the same way, company human resources representatives could gain access to your profile through someone else showing it to them and they could find all those drunken pictures you thought you'd cleverly hidden by making your profile private.

At a minimum, you might consider making your Facebook profile private and create a professional Facebook profile. To do this, use another version of your name or a different email to fit in with Facebook's rules. A professional profile allows you to accept your co-workers' friend requests and prevents any sort of awkward conversations about you not accepting their friend requests. Obviously, there's still a chance they'll know you have two profiles — but that's becoming more and more common these days. A similar effect can be achieved with Facebook's limited profile option, but with the company's frequent privacy setting changes, your profile might all of a sudden go public without you knowing.

Clean up your Google search results. To be reactive, you can google yourself regularly (or set up Google Alerts with your name) and deal with anything negative that comes up. To be proactive, don't do anything online or in person that could result in negative Google results when your name is searched, e.g. if you have a penchant for posting inflammatory comments on message boards, feel free, but maybe don't use your full name or anything related to it. Use a made-up handle instead.

20 Interviewing

Every heart sings a song, incomplete until another heart whispers back. Those who wish to sing always find a song.

— ANONYMOUS

It's a great idea to take workshops on how to interview. You can also do mock interviews.

For a behavioural interview (where they ask you questions about past examples of your behaviour, e.g. "What did you do when ____?"), or any type of interview, you can use the CAR method. By this I mean, if they ask you something, respond with Context, Action, and Results:

Example: "Tell me about a time when you grew a business."

Context: For context, it's good to provide a variety of positions you've held in your different answers, e.g. don't focus all answers on one specific job that you held — spread it out. The interviewers want a balance of leadership, work, and volunteer experience. You should spend minimal time on this part because you don't want to provide too much backstory before you move to the next section.

Action: In this section, talk about what you did. Try to attribute things to yourself as much as possible ("I did _____" versus "We did _____") for a more powerful impact (assuming it's true, of course!). Spend moderate time on this section.

Results: Here, provide the results that happened because of your action. Measurable results are best, since they have the most impact. You can spend lots of time on this section.

Keep your answers to two- to five-minute responses and don't be afraid to take time to think about the best answer before you launch into it. It's way better to come up with a good example rather than to start down a path with unclear/untruthful replies. Watch the body language of the interviewers and listen to their responses. If they're negative or off-putting during responses, consider cutting your replies shorter.

If they ask you about ideas for improvement for the company, make sure not to say anything too negative. Instead, add ideas incrementally.

At first, they'll probably ask you about yourself. Come out right off the bat with interests and good starters — first impressions are important. Along these lines, be nice to everyone you meet. The secretary might be asked to report back on your behaviour.

Most importantly, have the right mindset. In sales, we say, "Presume the close," e.g. presume you'll make the sale, or in this case, get the job. Be pumped so full of confidence that there's no way you're not going to get the job. Exude confidence. There are a couple of ways to get pumped up like this — for instance, before giving a speech I like playing a fun song and dancing to it. Approach the interview like a date — you're both getting to know each other.

If they ask you why you want to work with them, don't just talk about all the potential benefits to you. Let them know what skills you bring to the table and include what you can offer them in your answer.

If they ask about salary, you could say something like: "I was previously making _____" (or "My university prepared me with a figure of _____") … but I'm willing to be flexible because I really want this position." Let them know that compensation is important to you, but that it's not the be-all and end-all, because it shouldn't be. If it is, you can skip this book and make a beeline for investment banking.

Bring a list of questions to ask the interviewers that help you answer other questions for yourself later (an example being "Is the company a right fit for me?"). Don't ask about benefits, vacation, et cetera, in the first interview because they want to see that you're really interested in the company more than just the pay. You could ask things like: "What career paths are there to follow within the company?", "Are there any volunteer opportunities within the company?" It's also a good idea to do background research on the individuals who will be interviewing you so you can ask them details about their careers. You could say something like "Tell me about your career path. I'm interested in hearing how you started." People always love to talk about themselves, and interviewers are no exception.

At the end of the interview, shake hands, thank them, and ask for business cards if you don't have contact information. Follow up with a thank-you note for the opportunity to be interviewed.

A seemingly bad interview isn't the end of the world. It might even mean the interviewer liked you so much that he or she decided to test you. When the on-campus interviews rolled around at my school, I was pretty enthused that two things seemed to work strongly in my favour. First, I had to do my interview earlier than everyone else because the next day I was going to Ottawa to receive my Duke of Edinburgh from Prince Edward. Saying that you have a date with a prince is pretty much the best excuse you can ever give when asking to move a job interview to a different day. Second, one of the recruiters was pretty chill and loved the fact that I had a radio show, longboarded — things my classmates and I had previously thought would in no way benefit me in getting a job. Later, the interviewers told me they had benchmarked all the other candidates they'd interviewed that week against me.

For the next step, I travelled to Toronto for a day visit and interview at the corporate headquarters. While previously I'd been pretty blasé about whether I got the position or not, when I stepped into the office and saw all the beautiful decorations and products, I knew I wanted the position badly and began to get pretty nervous about the whole thing. When the end of the interview rolled around, I felt as if I totally blew it. While my on-campus interview had been extremely positive and affirming, I thought this interview was extremely negative, with questions mainly along the lines of "Tell us about a time when you failed and what you did about it," and more provocatively, "What was the biggest mistake you've ever made in your life?" There was one guy I was sure was giving me the evil eye the whole time, and the interviewers often asked me to re-answer a question because they thought the answer I'd given wasn't good enough or didn't answer their question properly. But I got the job. It turns out that maybe they were more on my side than I thought.

If you think you're not good at talking to people, go to Toastmasters International, a non-profit educational organization that operates clubs worldwide to help members improve communication, public-speaking, and leadership skills. A side note: it's been reported that Toastmasters' revenue for 2016 was $34.25 million.[1] Not bad for a non-profit! I've been to some Toastmasters meetings, and they're helpful for getting rid of those pesky likes, ums, and ahs.

Another idea to help make you quicker on your feet is to take improvisation classes. I've enjoyed and gained a lot of value from enrolling in improv classes at Second City. If you're feeling adventurous, try a stand-up comedy class! It often culminates in a performance and is great fun, plus great experience in learning how to make people laugh (it turns out there's a formula for everything). It might help you to roll with the punches in an interview. The best improv class I've found is Improv for Anxiety by Cameron Algie at Second City in Toronto. Cameron also runs his own classes and corporate gigs. Even if you don't have anxiety, these classes will help you to feel more comfortable making mistakes, and even to celebrate mistakes and laugh at yourself, in a nice way, when you make them. He's designed them in such a way that you can become more comfortable with any situation life throws your way, whether expected, or more likely, unexpected.

21 Make Your Own Job

One doesn't discover new lands without consenting
to lose sight, for a very long time, of the shore.

— ANDRÉ GIDE, *The Counterfeiters*

Not appetized by any of the job prospects out there? Prefer to do things
your own way? Then try entrepreneurship, the single best way I've found
to achieve my dreams. It's not for everyone. But for me, it's the main way
I've found that I can be happy at work. Why? I can do what I want! If I
stop liking an aspect of my role, I can change it and adapt it to my new
skills and interests. Working in a startup is much the same, provided,
of course, it has flexibility and a desire to help you grow and to grow
with you. As your skills improve and the company grows, why wouldn't
it advance you to help grow the company even further? That's if you're
performing well, obviously.

Entrepreneurship is also a great way to learn and stay inspired. I read
a *ton*, and it really helps me with running my own company. If I was
working at someone else's company, would I be as inspired to learn and

to grow? Maybe. But maybe not. On the other hand, I try to foster an environment that makes people excited to improve. And I've heard of companies that actually provide financial incentives for learning and growing as a staff member. If members of a team seem really excited about a task that could help expand the company, why not let them have at it? Doing so performs dual functions of bolstering the company and also making team members more excited and passionate, which in turn grows the company and its profits by keeping them around and making sure they're excited and engaged.

Here are some case examples from my own life. I joined a group within Entrepreneurs Organization, an international association for entrepreneurs with businesses above a certain size. Through the events and discussions I've had as part of this group, I've learned about countless useful books and resources that help transform businesses for the better. Whenever I discover a new resource that can assist my business, whether it be a book or a website, I'm motivated to seek it out and apply it. A recent example is Verne Harnish's book *Scaling Up*.[1] That book is like my business Bible right now. I'm digesting it at a rate of only a few pages per day, much slower than my average book consumption rate, because every page is like a truth bomb. And almost every chapter has links to other resources, e.g. books on specific topics. And each of *those* is amazing and recommends other resources that are equally epic. Furthermore, each page I digest is like going down a rabbit hole and not knowing when I'll come up. But the results of applying the disciplines recommended in Harnish's book have been tremendous. After utilizing the weekly meeting framework suggested in it, my team and I are solving more major issues now each week that might have otherwise bogged us down for months.

So the rhythm I've landed on goes a little something like this: learn about a resource, explore it, and apply it. Each item that I work on adds to the business for the better. Or if I'm facing an existing issue, I seek out the recommended resources to help fix it, explore them, and then apply them. I found out about the book *Who: The A Method for Hiring*[2] and its partner *Topgrading*[3] and used principles from them to help fix staffing issues that I had and hired new rock stars who made those issues seem like a forgotten nightmare. They've almost completely disappeared from my memory, since the new people I'm working with now are so great.

If you get sick of an aspect of your role as an entrepreneur, you can change it. A while ago I started to get burned out. I had too much on my plate, too many administrative items, and therefore too much stress. In a regular job, you might not have much flexibility to change your role. In a business you own, you can transform it almost entirely. There are some things you probably don't want to give up overseeing, like making sure taxes get paid (otherwise you're on the hook, my friend!). But many other things can be delegated, and some are better dealt with by others rather than you. I hired an incredible virtual assistant who took on a lot of the work I was too busy to do, and she ended up performing those tasks even better than I could have! And what's more, she did them faster! So we saved money all round and made more money because her efforts began to pay off quickly — and the work on my plate was reduced and I was less burned out and less stressed, too.

If you don't like something your own company does, you can change it. You could pivot the whole business if you wanted to. On a smaller level, you could decide to ditch certain service offerings or change the way your company does certain types of business. We initially did a weekly event we called "Open Make" in which kids could make whatever they wanted using items from our "wall of possibilities." It was a great idea in theory, but it didn't go well. With so many possibilities of activities to choose from, our staff were left trying to provide one-on-one instruction when the ratio was nowhere close enough to allow that to happen. Plus, sometimes tons of people showed up without booking, so we didn't have enough staff; other times, not many people came so we had too many employees there. In addition, we usually sold the items (e.g. pom poms) off the wall at or below cost because it seemed tricky to sell them for the typical three times the price to get a good margin, since it was so obviously much higher. And we had so many different items (maybe 200), which made it hard to keep track of prices, purchase items, and ensure restocking.

To make matters worse, customer satisfaction surrounding this event wasn't high. People didn't feel as if they got enough instructor time and were (rightly) confused about the prices of materials. All around, it was a risky event that was very stressful to run. So we got rid of it! And instantly, all that stress just *disappeared*. And as we focused on other areas (e.g. camps) that were more profitable and dependable, our business grew and more than made up for the losses associated with discontinuing this event. In fact, the mind share that was freed up by eliminating this stressful event came in handy for dreaming up new ideas to improve our other existing business lines. This is an example of how you, as an entrepreneur, can change your business to fit your goals.

As a CEO, if you want to do finance, do it! If you want to learn more about marketing, go for it. As long as it's in service of your business and the other functions can still reasonably get done, you're good. And that's how you can transform your business into something that services your dreams, goals, strengths, and aspirations. A business is like a tangible entity that you can transmute these things into. In a way, you can change *you* into it. That might sound weird, but I believe that a business is highly representative of the owner or entrepreneur because he or she necessarily creates much of what needs to go into it. For example, I've helped my team members figure out how to respond to certain inquiries, and now how we respond is largely based on my opinion and experience. So, in a way, for better or worse, your business becomes a representation of your personality. And in addition to that, it evolves into an entity that can serve you over time.

I used to think of myself and my business as inseparable, as if I *were* the business, as weird as that sounds. When I made decisions for the company, I made them based on whether it was best for me. But then after speaking with one of my mentors and doing some reading on the topic, I realized that a better way to perceive things was to think of the business as a third-party entity that both my team members and I worked for. So then instead of looking at decisions through the lens of how they affected me, I asked how they affected the company as a whole and everyone involved in it. But as the biggest shareholder, I can certainly still make decisions that benefit both me and others!

Your business can become a vehicle for change and growth that can reward you more and more based on the effort you put into it and the market forces co-operating along your journey. You can expand your business. You can multiply it. You can withdraw funds from it and put them toward purchasing your future house. You can control your compensation and tie it to the success of the company. It's all about your creativity, drive, and passion. And best of all, you can potentially put your strengths and interests to their best use in a business. Like the Burning Man example, running a business is like hanging your shingle out (or virtual shingle, if you prefer) and saying, "Hey, this is what I can offer you. Do you want it?" I believe that in its ideal form, it's offering the best of you and what you can do in order to benefit others.

You can use your business to provide happiness, fulfillment, or other forms of benefit to your customers. And from this, you'll derive happiness by knowing you helped contribute to theirs. You can meet friends, make acquaintances, and I believe, have the best chance of growing positively as a person. Now it's not easy. There are plenty of struggles, and I could talk your ears off about all the war stories and battle scars I have. But I won't, because I learned from them all, and that learning was worth the pain and risk of those negative experiences. They're notches on my victory belt. I don't think I could have grown personally anywhere near as much as I have through any other way.

Through your business, you can set an example. You can make a light that shines on others and encourages them to take the right action. For example, I had my business certified as a B Corporation. Being a B Corp is something I had read about for years — it's a designation for social-impact organizations that's hard to get but demonstrates that your for-profit company has objectives beyond solely profit maximization. This allows you to make decisions that, for instance, prioritize environmentally friendly choices over profit maximization and still be in good standing with shareholders. Etsy, Ben and Jerry's, Patagonia, and many other well-known brands are B Corps. From the moment I heard about it, I came to believe that this was the best way to do business. Rather than relying on grants — especially since reading up on grant economics shows the cost of applying for, delivering results on, and reporting on grants often exceeds the actual amount of money received — many B Corps sell services at full price and then use part of their profits to deliver services to underserved markets. This is the kind of company I want to build, and I tell anyone who will listen about the B Corp designation. Now those who visit our website and see the logo prominently displayed there, or those who hear about B Corps from me might consider certifying their businesses as B Corps, which might lead to more good in the world. This is an example of how you can use your business as a light that shines on others.

Another way you can do this is simply by starting the business and having people find out about it. People from your school, community, or even family might realize *they* can start a business, too, and might decide to go for it, all because they saw you do it! It's even better if your business becomes quite successful, which can help motivate others even more to create their own businesses. And in this process, perhaps they, too, will find more satisfying and fulfilling careers. As an added bonus, they might even become more pleasant at family holidays, gatherings of friends, and in their everyday life, which is all to your benefit, as well, especially if you're close to them!

So how do you transmute your strengths and desires into the real world? Start a business, of course!

22 What to Do When You Can't Decide

When one door closes, another opens; but we often look so long and so regretfully upon the closed door that we do not see the one which has opened for us.

— ALEXANDER GRAHAM BELL

It might seem as if there are too many options or that it's too hard to choose. You're not alone. Many of us go through "analysis paralysis," the process of not being sure what to choose and therefore choosing nothing. But the key is to pick *something* from the menu of options you have in front of you. Otherwise, what are you really doing? I recently met with a dean from a nearby university who told me that one of their students got a three-month contract with a big company that was an industry leader, but because it was three months and there might not be a job left for him at the end, he decided to work at Starbucks instead. *Really?* But what can you do about that? Done is better than best, and perfect is the enemy of done. *Just choose something. Just choose something. Just choose something.*

Because otherwise what are we actually doing? It's better to be out there in the world doing *something* and learning from it than sitting alone on your couch watching that episode of *Girls* for the fifth time. Because what can you learn from that other than that Lena Dunham is a terrific writer?

In contrast, think of all you could learn from a day on the job. Even a retail store has plenty of learning to offer, though you might not think so initially. How are the training manuals laid out? How do instructions get transferred from store to store? Why is the store laid out the way it is? This is all very fruitful information that could be used quite effectively if applied to something related, such as franchising. So as much as I'm an advocate of trying to get the best job you can, I don't necessarily recommend holding out too long or choosing sitting on a couch as a strategy rather than getting out there and doing work and contributing to society. After all, isn't that what all of us have the responsibility to do? Providing we have the physical and mental capacity to do it, of course, I think we should work or figure out another way to contribute to society in a meaningful way. Even if you later decide to remove a job from your résumé, working can be good. That being said, if you have a meaningful idea and plan for what you want to do during time off, and the wherewithal to stick to it, by all means. A meditation retreat or a multi-week shadowing plan are good examples. But if you intend to use the time to sleep or watch television, consider thinking again, unless you really need a good vacation, that is.

If I'm interviewing people, and I see they haven't worked for the past year, and when I ask them why, they say, "I left because I didn't like it. Since then I've been applying to jobs, and the job market is tough, and I'm being selective," I get a little nervous. If I ask them what else they've been doing and they say something like, "Oh, you know, watching comedy videos on YouTube," I'm ready to tear their résumés into a million little pieces, but not in front of them, of course. But if they give a good answer that highlights their capacity for personal growth, such as they used the time to teach themselves to code and then they follow that up with showing me a website they've built, I'm impressed.

In the chart on the next page, let's examine the pros and cons of working in a job that might not be ideal:

Pros of Working in a Job that Might Not Be Ideal	Cons of Working in a Job that Might Not Be Ideal
• Build your résumé. • Build professional contacts. • Gain experience. • Build up savings. • Less time to worry.	• Might dislike it so much that you might underperform and burn your bridges. • Potential for constant worry about whether or not this is what you should be doing.

FIG. 17: *The pros and cons of working in a job that might not be ideal.*

It's all a balance of probabilities, and there's no right answer. In the end, it's up to you to decide.

For whatever reason, if all else fails and you can't change jobs, consider the following. I went to a talk about Steve Jobs and Buddhism, and one of the topics discussed was: "What is work?" The speaker posited that there's no such thing — it's a misunderstanding. He said it should be an activity you're passionate about and that you'd do without hesitation. Choosing to do it makes it work. He said that in an enlightened life it should be the same for any activity, that activities shouldn't be viewed as positive or negative but instead as "this is what I'm doing now" and "I don't care if it's this or that — it's just what I'm doing." Most people don't get lucky enough to find the work they love, so just choose the best thing you can.

In the end, it's important to use your intuition to make decisions, which will help guide you to incredible life experiences, ones that help you grow. Take advantage of serendipitous opportunities; serendipity is your friend. Things might arrive in your life at the exact time you need them. Make sure you keep your eyes open and don't let these special moments pass you by.

Once you've made your decision, it's time for no regrets. Don't be sorry about the decision you've made and don't regret all the time you spent at the job you didn't enjoy. It's a "sunk cost" now. What's a sunk cost? Good question. In economics, a sunk cost is one that's already been spent and can't be recovered. In business, it means not making a decision based on those you've made previously. In life, it means not spending more time on something because you've done it before. In other words, just because you've always played tennis, doesn't mean you should *keep* doing it if you're starting to get sick of it. The fact that you've played tennis for so long is near-irrelevant in the face of all the potential years in the future you could devote to a different sport. Don't keep playing tennis because you feel you *should* in order to make use of the time you did it in the past. Otherwise, as I heard one therapist put it, you're merely "should-ing all over yourself."

In a similar vein, I don't think it's healthy or productive to actively regret things you've done in the past. What good will that do? It will only make you feel bad. Instead, I prefer an approach where I think to myself, *Okay, I did that, and I don't want to do that again. That's okay, though. I'm glad I learned that.* Sometimes, even if something in life seems entirely negative, it can actually be something positive in disguise. If all of life were positive, how would we differentiate or even feel our "up" emotions, e.g., happiness, giddiness? Everything would be the same, and everything would be flat. Life would be mediocre. Thus, it's my belief that the bad exists to highlight the good. Negative experiences fuel our creativity and serve to enhance our bonds with others — after all, we often need someone to talk to about them.

23 For Students

Twenty years from now you'll be more disappointed by the things you didn't do than by the ones you did. So throw off the bowlines. Sail away from the safe harbor. Catch the trade wind in your sails. Explore. Dream. Discover.

— ANONYMOUS

If you're a student, this is such a pivotal moment in your life — the choices you make now will have a profound impact going forward. So I want to share a few lessons I learned, things that helped me along the way to where I am now, and things I wish I'd known when I was a student that might help you be more successful in your career — and entrepreneurship, if you choose.

BEING A STUDENT IS LIKE A SHIELD

You have so much freedom to try what you want to do without a gaping hole in your résumé. At the moment, it might be hard to see school as much more than marks, extracurriculars, and optimizing your experience so you can "get into" the next thing, but looking back I see university as a time to really explore what you want to do and to garner some early success in that area before jumping off the cliff that is graduation. Because once you graduate, you won't have as many resources or as much support, and there will be a lot of pressure not to leave a hole in your résumé to explore. So what I tried to do during university was take advantage of every single thing it offered me, from business plan competitions, to student awards, to conferences, professor advice, and travel opportunities — you name it. It's not all about marks. In fact, in my career coaching, I've noticed that in most cases marks don't matter when getting a job; it's more about leadership experience, with a few exceptions, like accounting and consulting. If you want to start a company, doing so in university is a great time to act. You're eligible for all sorts of awards, can get your professors to give you advice without them charging you consulting fees, and many successful businesses started this way. Think Facebook and Google. Plus, you can reach out to successful people, companies, and competitors under the guise of a "student project" or as a soon-to-graduate student investigating the possibility of a career in their industries. So take advantage of your time as a student. Prolong it if needed.

When I was a student, I thought taking a gap year would set me back. Now I realize that's completely not true. I have friends who did a gap year before university or managed to convince their employers to let them take a year off after university before starting working (much harder) and used that time to travel or experiment with other jobs. When else in your life will you be able to spend months at a time travelling solo in another part of the world? Certainly not when you're married, have kids, and a thriving career. By taking the time off to reflect, you'll actually be farther ahead than your peers. You'll have a clue about what you want to do in life. And there are lots of programs and financial aid available for travel.

Something a lot of people don't realize until too late is the importance and value of summer internships. If you end up graduating without work experience, it might be difficult to get a job or start a successful business right away. That's why it's important to get the best summer jobs you can as early as possible. The better the first job that you get is, the better your subsequent summer jobs and ultimate full-time position will be. And don't assume you can't find something just because you're young. You can get sweet gigs right now. I've met people who worked at the Stanford d.school and at Apple's headquarters while they were still in high school. Or you can try your hand at a full-time entrepreneurship during the summer and secure funding for it from programs such as the Next 36, My Summer Company, or your school. Now that you know that the label *student* is a shield, my next tip is to ...

PICK YOUR PROGRAM AND SCHOOL CAREFULLY

This might sound obvious, but there's some not-so-obvious things to consider. Pick the best school you can get into. When I was choosing schools, I thought about whether I wanted to be a big fish in a little pond or a little fish in a big pond, e.g. the smartest in the class or somewhere in the middle or near the bottom. Now I realize that some recruiters only go to certain schools, and it's way better to do okay at an amazing school than to be outstanding at an okay school. The okay schools simply don't have the alumni, street cred, or resources that better schools possess.

Another thing to consider (if you still have time to apply to schools and if you're able to) is to submit applications to places where you're not sure you'll get accepted. I got into all the schools I applied to but I didn't apply to Stanford or Harvard, so now I'll never know if I would have gotten in. I might have been rejected, but even if I did get turned down, I still could have gone to the schools I applied to in the first place. So why not throw a ticket into the lottery, so to speak? What's the worst that could happen?

You should also know that business school isn't necessarily required to launch a business. Many famous founders, such as Jack Dorsey (Twitter),

Mark Zuckerberg (Facebook), Larry Ellison (Oracle), and Travis Kalanick (Uber), didn't go to business school ... or even finish university! In some ways, I think business school can actually harm your prospects of being an entrepreneur — it's *really* hard not to take a job when you see all your classmates signing with companies at $60,000 to $100,000 plus per year. Only one other classmate of mine (that I know of) from the 300 in my year in Queen's Commerce is also pursuing entrepreneurship full-time. And you don't *really* need to know all that detail about business to start one. If I were embarking on university now, I'd strongly consider something like a computer science or engineering degree, or something else I'm interested in. That being said, some degrees simply don't lead to jobs unless you really, really work at it. China recently got rid of a lot of their degree programs that weren't leading to employment. The last thing to know about education is around this quote, which is often erroneously attributed to Mark Twain: "I never let my schooling interfere with my education." Recognize that schools teach based on information from at least one to two years ago (if not 20 years ago or more!), but things are changing all the time. So you need to supplement your university education beyond your classes. Examples: articles, keeping a blog, extracurriculars, job shadowing, et cetera.

FORGET HIGH SCHOOL: IT DOESN'T MATTER ANYMORE

This might be hard to read, but don't bother putting high school on your résumé or mentioning it in interviews. What you did in high school helped get you into the university and program you're in now. That means companies can reasonably assume you and the rest of your classmates did similar things in high school to get accepted. Now it's about differentiating yourself based on your experiences and accomplishments at university.

MARKS DON'T MATTER (WITH SOME EXCEPTIONS)

Find out what your desired profession/company expects and work toward it, e.g. by taking on leadership positions or doing whatever's most important in the field. This might surprise you, but marks don't matter as much as you think they do. Of course, they're important for getting into graduate school and certain professions such as consulting and accounting, but you should know that a very large proportion of companies never actually consider your marks when deciding whether or not to hire you. The consumer packaged goods company I worked for never did. And why should it? Studies have consistently shown that marks aren't a good predictor of job performance.[1] They're just numbers. I'm not saying you should stop doing your assignments — it's important to maintain a reasonable, at or above-average level of performance — but don't beat yourself up to become top of your class. Even if companies do look at your marks, if given the choice between someone with a 99 percent average and no social skills and someone with 80 percent and a strong record of leadership, most companies will go for the second candidate. The sooner you realize there are some things more important than marks, the sooner you'll begin focusing on the things that can *really* help you get the jobs you want.

EXTRACURRICULARS AND LEADERSHIP DO MATTER

Run conferences and competitions. Take on leadership positions. Companies care about these types of things.

SUMMER INTERNSHIPS MATTER

I have a theory that, in general, the better your internships, the better your final job will end up being. With each progressive internship you do, you become more qualified to land better positions during subsequent summers, and ultimately, after you graduate. My first internship, a marketing position with my university, gave me a distinct leg up in landing my internship with the consumer packaged goods company the following summer because I could show them a portfolio of samples of the work I'd done. When it came time to get a job after graduation, the company I'd worked with during my last internship hired me.

Many people secure jobs after graduation with companies they interned with because internships are perfectly conducive to it. As a CEO I know stated, an internship is like the courtship period in dating. The company and the intern go through a series of "dates" during the summer to determine if they like each other enough to take the relationship to the next level. If given the opportunity to hire someone who interned with a company and has a track record of success or someone random whom team members know very little about, a company will likely choose the intern. That's not to say you have to intern with a firm to get a job there. It's just that doing internships period will give you a major advantage. Using a similar scenario, a company will likely choose someone who's been hired for internships by other companies (preferably similar ones, whether by industry or size) over someone who has never had any professional internships at all. I've heard of a few people who obtained stellar jobs with major companies upon graduation after spending their summers tanning, but by far those are the exceptions rather than the rule. Plus, even after one year of university, you're qualified for a much higher pay rate than what you've experienced thus far. You might argue that you want to spend your last few summers having fun in the job you had before you started university, but don't forget to consider the benefits of doing professional internships. Higher pay and a higher chance of getting employed doing something you love after you graduate (since companies look for professional progression)? The choice, at least for me, was obvious.

INFO SESSIONS ROCK

Start attending info sessions as early as possible. I started in first-year university. Go to as many as you can — all industries, positions, and careers — until you've narrowed down what you're specifically looking for. Considering that many info sessions offer free food (and sometimes booze), it's a pretty good use of your time.

How I came to join the corporate world is a funny story and illustrates a mix of luck and gaming the system called life. Sometime during first year, my printer broke and I ended up spending a lot of time studying and printing notes in the Commerce computer lab where a lot of older students hung out and talked and where I eventually ended up taking a part-time job. Through overhearing conversations, I concluded that now that I had landed my extracurricular frosh rep positions, the next step on my path to success was securing a good internship as early as possible. This would increase my chances of getting subsequent internships at bigger companies and ultimately help me get the best job possible upon graduation.

At the same time, I discovered that most of the info sessions that companies were holding on campus included food, and quite often, drinks. So during the first few weeks of my first and second years, while most of my classmates weren't even thinking about jobs or their futures, I wore business casual every day and attended as many company info sessions as I could, sometimes two or three in one night, so that I could get as much free food, drinks, and learning as possible. Free dinner a couple of nights a week for the first few months of each school year wasn't too shabby, and I continued wearing business casual every day during the fall semester just in case.

My department also included a communications workshop series on a range of topics such as résumés, cover letters, and interviews. Although we were only required to attend a small number of these, I went to as many as possible and still consider them to be one of the most valuable aspects of my university education. I even won an award at my graduation ceremony for attending the most workshops. It turned out I was involved in triple the number of workshops required to graduate, and though many of my classmates chuckled at this, I was quite proud of myself. I still use the information I learned in these workshops to coach others in finding a job.

For the summer after my first year, I got a marketing position at my university. Although many people told me it wasn't possible to secure a good internship until after the third year, and the position description said the background required was "Some experience with, or understanding of, the higher education sector, some marketing and communications experience, and/or a relevant post-secondary education," which I had very little of, I decided to apply, anyway, and got the position. This experience proved extremely valuable in nailing down my internship the following summer with the big fish — a large corporation.

YOU HAVE TO DO THINGS DIFFERENTLY FROM THOSE AROUND YOU

As I've mentioned, you can prototype your career. John Krumboltz, who teaches career counselling at Stanford University, suggests making a list of the top things you think you might be interested in and then trying them out. Once you've done that, you can start to understand if you actually do enjoy them or not, instead of attempting predictions about it. Check out what Maeghan Smulders did with Project 112 (maeghansmulders.com/project/intern) — you can make your own self-education program that involves shadowing or short internship experiences at a variety of companies. Think about what you love, what your attention has always naturally been drawn to, and how you want the world to change. But know that you don't have to figure everything all out now.

PROTOTYPE

The education that stuck with me the most from university was what I learned from organizing events during my free time. This taught me most of what I needed to know about budgeting costs, time management, catering to egos (when working with a team), negotiation (with neighbours when they wanted to call the cops on us if the late-night event was getting too loud), marketing, and many more. I still use all these skills today, years after graduation day!

During my last week of final exams in university, because of scheduling reasons, I had finished way before my colleagues. With nothing else to do, I emailed 15 close friends and asked whether I could sit in on one of their last lectures before the holidays. To my surprise, many welcomed me with open arms. I was a business major and suddenly found myself in a whole new world of final-year-level computer programming, engineering, education, history, and physics classes. The experience opened my eyes to the questions: "How are we supposed to decide what we want to dedicate ourselves to for the next 30 to 40 years?" and "How do these people know so confidently there isn't another option that better fits their personalities, strengths, and abilities?"

My biggest regret was that I didn't drop into various lectures like this every couple of months during my four years because I was too busy "getting an education."

CHOOSING A UNIVERSITY AND A PROGRAM

For me, when it came to figuring out where to go to university and what to major in, I definitely had a hard time deciding. While I'd always thought I wanted to go to the same university that my parents attended (the University of Western Ontario), I began to doubt whether that was really what I wanted and whether I'd be able to get in. Self-doubt and indecision set in, and I made sure to apply to a variety of schools on the spectrum of low tier to high tier to make sure I'd have *somewhere* to go. I ended up getting in everywhere I applied, but for some reason I wasn't confident that I would at the time I applied. I actually almost didn't write the secondary application required for the school I did go to — Queen's University. In my high-school brain, I thought the fact that they required a personal statement of experience essay (while most other schools only wanted to see your grades) was a bit snobby and uncalled for. Later, I realized this admission criteria was precisely what made it the best school for me.

To help me with my decision, I frequented the forums on a website called Scholarships Canada (scholarshipscanada.com). I'd already done career coaching and personality testing (thanks to my amazing parents hooking me up with that!) to narrow my choices for what to major in down to business or arts, but I wasn't sure which one or which school to go for. On this website, I was able to ask current students my burning questions — Western Ivey or Queen's Commerce? What should I include in my application for specific scholarships? It was extremely helpful. When it came time to pick a school, I selected the business program at Western and was pretty sure I was going to go there. But at the very last minute before the deadline, I changed my mind and switched to Queen's.

A few minutes after the midnight deadline had passed, I let my parents know. I'd just felt in my heart a stronger feeling about Queen's, and that was definitely enhanced by the discussions I'd had with graduates from each program. While folks from Western spoke about the program along the lines of "Yeah, it's good; it's a lot of hard work, though," the people I met from Queen's were like "Yes, you have to do this! It will be the best decision you've ever made in your life!"

Choosing Queen's was one of the best decisions I ever made, and I've used the decision-making heuristic of "going where the passion is" successfully many times since. While I was a bit worried the classmates I'd have would be overly snobby and/or nerdy, I was pleasantly surprised to discover that most of them were very much like me. It was the perfect place for me. I'd thought about applying to universities in the United States but never did because my parents told me I'd probably only get to see them once a year at Christmas. I think going to school a couple of hours away from home was a great balance. I was able to see them every so often, and we were close enough that I could make it home or they could make it to me in around four hours by bus, train, or car.

My final thoughts on the matter:

- You're young.
- Take risks — a concept we learned in finance is that more risks equal more rewards. This also applies to life. And youth is the perfect time to make mistakes.
- Avoid debt like the plague. It limits your options.
- Think about what stuff you can do *now* that you won't be able to do later and then do those things!
- Go where the fun is.

24 Make Your Own Blueprint

> There is no map, and charting a path ahead will not be easy. We will need to invent, which means we will need to experiment.
>
> — JEFF BEZOS

A CHECK-IN: THE BEST BLUEPRINT IN LIFE IS THERE IS NO BLUEPRINT

I once read an article entitled "A Blueprint for a Woman's Life." I've read a lot of articles similar to it, ones that purport a certain sequence of steps to get to a certain level of accomplishment in life. I'm here to tell you that I wholeheartedly disagree with these kinds of blueprints.

Let's take the example of becoming a venture capitalist (VC), something I'm potentially interested in doing eventually. The "blueprint," as I've read it, is: (1) start a startup; (2) sell your startup; and (3) become a VC. However, through looking at different VC job postings, I noticed that some of their requirements are actually quite different: (1) go to a top-tier M.B.A. school; (2) work in a major management consulting or investment banking firm; and (3) become a VC. The point is, there are different routes to becoming a VC, and you shouldn't follow one just to get to the end goal. You should do what makes you happy the whole way through, or as much as possible.

And then there's the example of becoming an entrepreneur. While I was in school, I was told that the recipe for becoming an entrepreneur was: (1) finish university; (2) work for a big company for a few years; (3) start a startup; and (4) profit. Well, it turns out you don't need lots of work experience to run a successful startup. You don't even need a university degree. In fact, some of the most successful entrepreneurs have little to no work experience or a university degree!

I think these blueprints people push on others are dangerous. They might cause, for example, a young university student to mistakenly think she needs corporate experience to become a successful entrepreneur, even though she has a pretty good idea and she won't like the corporate world. Sound familiar? If I could go back in time, I might not have gone to my corporate job following graduation. I could have created the startup I had plans for, validation of, and funding offers for. Because I can honestly say I don't see a huge amount about that job that helped me with becoming a successful entrepreneur. In fact, I sometimes wonder if it might have hindered my abilities. Why? Because I wasn't really learning the key skills to becoming an entrepreneur. I was mostly learning to follow the rules, keep my head down, debate minuscule decisions for weeks or months on end, complain about decisions outside our office's control, and create one-pagers according to a meticulous format requirement that even specified the font and size of the text.

None of those skills are applicable to being a successful entrepreneur. In fact, they're the opposite of what you should do. And when I went down to Silicon Valley, boy, was I shocked to learn that very few people I spoke to valued my corporate experience. Some of them actually perceived it as a negative thing, saying I was a "big-company person" and might not know how to operate in a small company. I guess the fact that I quit fairly early could actually be a good thing.

ARE YOU A STOCK OR A BOND?

Someone sent me an article about entrepreneurial DNA recently, and I find it very relevant to my situation.[1] It says people are naturally like an equity (more risky) or a bond (more risk-averse) and that business school has a habit of changing people from equities into bonds. It's true. I think business school mesmerized me. Before university, I thought I'd do non-profit work after graduation. I never dreamed I'd instead take a job pushing detergent. But it seemed to be the thing to do according to the environment I was in for those four years. However, when I got out of school and into the actual thick of the work, I began to realize I still wanted to do the same non-profit/altruistic stuff I'd originally intended to do.

I'm hesitant to do my M.B.A. for a number of reasons, but a major one is that I don't want to get mesmerized again. I don't want to be pushed toward the corporate world so the school can keep up its re-cruiting statistics and corporate sponsorships. I'm seeing a lot of friends and acquaintances who used to be very entrepreneurial in corporate jobs that they hate. But they stay. The companies are helping them finish the job their business schools started by transforming them fully from an equity into a bond. The minute my friends begin to look sad or seem as if they're searching elsewhere, the companies put a carrot in front of their faces — a raise, promotion, car, or free M.B.A. — and they decide to stay. And I know from experience that being surrounded by very risk-averse people every day in companies like those ones makes it very hard to extract yourself from the situation. After all, are people who made a decision to stay there for years despite their unhappiness going to advise you otherwise? (Well, actually, some did at my job, and then I *really* knew it was time to quit.)

Anyway, my advice to everyone trying to follow a "blueprint" from their parents, co-workers, career counsellors, or articles is to *snap out of it now!* Instead, follow your own path. Even though what I'm doing now is way riskier than ever before, I'm so much happier because I know the potential payoff is way greater than the potential downside.

25 Prototyping Life

Not everything that is faced can be changed. But nothing can be changed until it is faced.

— JAMES BALDWIN

I wrote this book about prototyping your career, but the reality is that you can apply the tools and principles to virtually any area of your life. Trying to decide where to live? Try out a few different places. Attempting to choose a school? Spend a day at each. Figuring out what you're looking for in a romantic partner? You know what to do.

All jokes aside, prototyping your options is the best method I've found to choose an option that's most likely the best outcome for you. I've prototyped my life outside work in a variety of different ways. Here are some of them.

WHERE TO LIVE

I feel as if I was born with a touch of wanderlust. My parents were gracious enough to take my brother and I travelling a fair amount, and when it came time to select a university, the ability to go on exchange was high on my list of criteria. Once I did so, I was hooked. I chose my exchange destination based on which had the best kiteboarding, and of course, which had the best academic reputation. The answer was Perth, Australia. While there, I made an effort to ascertain what all aspects of living entailed Down Under. I took holidays at my Australian friends' houses and stuck around for the "cold weather" season, discovering that it really *is* cold and rainy, much to this Canadian's surprise. Worse, only a few houses have heating, so it was pretty much colder than I'd ever experienced indoors.

Then I decided to try a few other places: Sri Lanka, Malaysia, Singapore, Indonesia, Hong Kong, San Francisco, and eventually Chile. I was lucky to have the time and budget to take these trips; after graduation I had a few months off before my job started and I wanted to travel to Asia. I knew I had an abundance of free time — possibly more than I'd ever have again — but not an abundance of money. In other words, I was broke. But with my shiny new contract in hand, I was able to convince a bank to give me a loan, and promptly used that to travel.

I don't recommend this for everyone. For example, if my job offer had been cancelled for some reason (such as downsizing), I would have been sunk. But luckily the job and company were stable enough that I was reasonably sure they'd be around when I returned. Travel doesn't have to be super-expensive. You can wander around Southeast Asia for as little as $10 per day or possibly even less, yet live like a king (or queen). And you can also try couchsurfing. For those who haven't heard of it, couchsurfing is a worldwide movement in which people offer up their couches for international travellers to stay. But instead of being based on payment, like Airbnb, it has more to do with karma. I couchsurfed extensively when I explored living in California, and later hosted couchsurfers while I lived in Chile in an effort to pay it forward. I tried Palo Alto, Mountain View, and different parts of San Francisco, deciding that ultimately I wanted to spend some time in Palo Alto, which I did a few years later once I got a U.S. visa.

You don't necessarily need a whole lot of time to determine whether or not you might like to live in a place. The key is to spend time living like a local and doing all the things you might need to do. Once I began living in the United States, I got a library card, social security number, and doctor. It was through this process that I realized I much preferred living in Canada. In retrospect, before applying for a visa, it might have been good to try out these basic everyday tasks while I was visiting California — but I likely wouldn't have been able to do all of them without the visa.

There are great opportunities out there for funded international travel. Whether it's a work opportunity, job interview, travel writing, or humanitarian work, it's amazing how you can be creative to get to a country of interest more cheaply. I came across the Start-Up Chile program, which offered $40,000 for selected foreign entrepreneurs to live and work in Chile for six months in exchange for mentoring Chileans and contributing to the local entrepreneurial environment. I jumped at the chance. I'd always wanted to spend six months in South America and learn Spanish, and now here was my opportunity to do so — and be paid for it! I highly recommend this program or others like it, since it's a great way to experience a new and different business environment and decide whether it's somewhere you might like to stay for the long term.

For me, I followed a path similar to this T.S. Eliot quote from "Little Gidding": "We shall not cease from exploration / And the end of all our exploring / Will be to arrive where we started / And know the place for the first time." After all that travelling, I realized the best place for me was right back where I started — back in Ontario. While some might think this experience — living in different countries to see where I wanted to live — was a waste of time if I ended up back in Toronto, anyway, I strongly disagree. I'm happy I spent the time and money to figure it out because I feel so much more strongly rooted in Canada as a result. Some people know in their hearts where they want to be without ever experiencing anywhere else. But for me, I needed to go out, explore, and prototype before declaring where I wanted to be and sticking my flag in the sand, so to speak.

LIVING ARRANGEMENTS

It might seem to some that the only living arrangement is the one we commonly see today — people living alone, with their families, or with roommates. But there are a growing number of what's called *intentional communities* where people do just what the term sounds like: live intentionally. I was fortunate enough to come across some of these communities in Palo Alto, which is partly why I ended up loving the city so much. I'd met a woman in Hong Kong at a concert, and when I was first visiting California, she was one of the only people I knew there at the time. I ended up going to stay with her, and when I arrived at her home, I felt as if I'd entered a completely different land.

Her home was a large housing structure with many rooms, and the residents cooked together, gardened together, and even sang together. I ended up being lucky enough to live in two of these "co-ops" during my time in California, and upon further investigation, I realized there were many different models of housing that could be better for some people rather than the traditional living arrangements. For example, in Denmark there's a proliferation of "cohousing" — apartment buildings where families have separate apartments but they take turns cooking in a communal commercial kitchen and share other chores. Each family cooks dinner once a month, and there's a set dinnertime when all the families come and enjoy the food that's cooked for them. In the Danish movie *Happy*, residents from a cohousing building talk about how much they love this sense of community and how it saves them each a few hours a day. Denmark is acknowledged as one of the happiest places in the world, and it's said to be partly because so many of their residents are in cohousing.

My own experience living in co-ops was fantastic and led me directly to choose the type of housing arrangement I'm in now. The first co-op consisted of three houses on the same plot of land, with a small backyard connecting all of them. Twelve of us lived there. We had chickens in the backyard, we hosted parties together, and we ate dinner together every night, with the possibility of a "late plate" if you were getting home after the set dinnertime. We each had roles, such as "social coordinator" or "chicken minder," and this was a way of ensuring everyone in the house contributed.

The second co-op had a number of houses associated with it and is considered a pioneer in the development of co-op housing policies and procedures. By the time I became involved, there was an elaborate system of points, voting, rules, and purchasing. Everything was thought out to the *T*. I loved it. Most of the residents were Stanford students and alumni who were an amazing mix of intelligence and alternative/hippie personalities. Case example: when a debate arose about what level we should keep the heat at, I was delighted to receive a detailed email with an analysis of the situation from an environmental engineering student, complete with regression models! We had a "free store" where we left articles of clothing and furniture we no longer needed and then "shopped" from those that had been left by others. We had a job system that sorted each "job," e.g. cleaning the kitchen, by points based on time commitment, pleasantness, and other factors. So, for instance, doing the dishes after two meals (often a one-hour task twice a week) could be considered equivalent to cleaning the washroom for half an hour once a week, because cleaning the washroom was rightly considered a less enjoyable, desired, and pleasant task.

We partied together, carpooled to San Francisco together, and maintained an active email group that contained offerings ranging from rides to doing hula-hooping in the living room. There were many different shared areas, such as an exercise/yoga room that sometimes functioned as a concert room, workshop, hangout area, bulk-food storage place, picnic tables for meal seating outdoors, laundry room, and more. Everything was well thought out with policies and instructions, but ones that made you feel expansive and excited rather than restricted.

There was a voting system in the weekly house meetings in which you could vote on a proposed motion with one to five fingers on one of your hands. Five meant "I'm all for it." One meant "I'm so against this that I'll move out if it passes." And you had to be willing to live up to that. I felt this was a great way to separate out the seriousness of various arguments. As well, any issues raised were immediately moved from discussion to proposed solutions in order to maintain a bias toward action. Instead of allowing an issue to be repeatedly discussed again and again in the same ways, people were given an opportunity to quickly voice opinions and then afterward the group was polled for proposed solutions. Then it was time to vote! I thought this was a fantastic way to ensure things didn't stagnate or get repeated too much, and to leave each one-hour meeting with concrete actions and take-homes. I ended up bringing this learning back to my business. At the co-op, the meeting leaders rotated and there was no official "leader" of the co-op. Instead, it was more of a democracy or a do-ocracy.

Prior to being in a co-op, I lived by myself or with roommates. I also tried these formats again after living in the co-op but realized I was looking for something that was the best of both worlds: a little communal but also with the time and space available for me to refresh myself solo.

In my life today, I've employed some of the aspects of group living that I experienced in California and some of my experience living solo. I found an amazing six-unit apartment building where despite the fact that the units are separate, we residents often hang out, trade items back and forth, and generally have one another's backs. For me, this is the perfect mix of solitary time and group time and support.

What kind of living arrangement is best for you?

RELATIONSHIP STYLES

I won't spend too long on this topic, but suffice to say, there are different types of romantic relationships you can explore. With 50 percent of marriages ending in divorce, you might decide the typical model isn't for you. More and more women these days are contemplating or going for single motherhood via sperm banks, adoption, or other means. They might find a partner later or they might not. Others explore different relationship models, whether it be polyamory, triads, open relationships, or a new term that has emerged *monogamish*. Still, others decide to be single and are happy with that decision. It could be that the traditional model of a romantic relationship is right for you, but it might be worth exploring whether that's really what *you* want or if it's just what you think society wants for you. A good way to explore this is to read books on the subject (such as *More Than Two*[1]) and talk with people pursuing alternative models of partnering, many of which are becoming more and more mainstream.

FOOD

What sort of diet is best for you? What energizes you and what depletes your energy? These are all important questions to answer and the responses can benefit you in many areas of your life, from career to personal. A great way to experiment with this is to use methods from the quantified self movement to prototype which foods are best for you and at what times. If you research quantified self plus food, you'll find websites, devices, and even apps that let you do things like take a picture of your food and receive back an estimate of the amount of calories it contains.

I've experimented with a number of different diets, and by that I mean eating regimens, not necessarily the typical weight-reducing diets commonly known. Once, I even tried eating mainly pizza and ice cream for a month. Believe it or not, I actually lost weight! But I'm pretty sure it was just muscle loss, and clearly the number on the scale isn't the only thing that matters. It's also about how much the food nourishes you, sustains you, and gives you energy. And it's different for every person!

For me, I've realized through experimentation that caffeine isn't a positive thing to have in my life. I much prefer to roll with my natural energy rather than artificially induced energy bursts that often lead to crashes later. But it's different for everyone! I've realized my body is quite sensitive, so caffeine hits me quite hard. This isn't the case for everybody. I also found that I feel best when I eat very regularly, i.e., when I never let myself go hungry. Others thrive on the caveman diet (in which you only eat once a day), but my MO is healthy food on a regular basis throughout the day. And I love lots of veggies and legumes for a regular diet — plus meats around once a week.

I've borrowed suggestions from Tim Ferriss's book *The 4-Hour Body*, which I highly recommend.[2] I also shadowed my awesome friend Ana as she shopped at a nearby healthy supermarket — and my friend Kunal as he made Ayurvedic food. I wouldn't say grocery shopping is something that comes very naturally to me, so it was helpful to see Ana's selection process and pick out a few things of my own at the same time. I also audited an amazing nutrition class at Stanford University led by the eminent scientist Clyde Wilson. This was a great way to learn about how different types of foods affect you and the science behind this process. One of the biggest takeaways for me was that if you're prone to binging on a huge tub of ice cream, it's better to allow yourself a spoonful every day or a few times a day in order to provide reasonable satisfaction rather than depriving yourself and then later binging on a huge amount of ice cream to make up for it.

EXTRACURRICULARS

I believe it's important to have extracurriculars, e.g. hobbies you do outside work that aren't job-related. Whether it's volunteering or joining a band, it can be great to prototype what sorts of extracurriculars are best for you. You might find that extracurriculars actually add more fuel and energy back into your life and help you to be more productive rather than take away time from your work — because you're having fun outside your employment.

One of my favourite extracurriculars is improv. I knew that I liked theatre and performance and then I tried different roles and formats within them and realized improv is one of my favourite forms of artistic expression.

What extracurriculars are best for you? Some people say they don't know where to start, but you can use the prototyping process to figure it out. Maybe instead of signing up for eight weeks of a topic you're not sure you'll like, you might try a one-night workshop in it and see if you want to proceed. Then, once you've chosen a specific area of interest, maybe you'll want to prototype different places to do that extracurricular. For example, I've tried improv in a few places, but my favourite venue is Second City in Toronto, which has managed to establish an incredible community. I love going to classes there and then hanging out with new friends afterward.

RELIGION AND SPIRITUALITY

This might be a controversial topic depending on your belief system, but I've also prototyped my religion and spirituality. What I mean by this is the following: I've tried adopting different beliefs and practices to see what fits with me. I visited various religious ceremonies and read books in order to learn more. My resultant spirituality is a cornucopia of ideas borrowed from different religions and spiritual disciplines. I attended Burning Man in Nevada, and that was a mind-opening experience. Many people think Burning Man is all about drugs, but I didn't take any or even drink and I had the most amazing experience. It's basically like the biggest culture shock I've ever experienced, despite the fact that I've been to a lot of far-off places. Where else can you walk down the street and have people approach and say hi, and offer you a mango slice? Nowhere that I've experienced! Where else can you go up to your neighbour who you've never met and ask to borrow a hammer and have that be a perfectly socially acceptable thing to do? It's no wonder so many people attend Burning Man, including tech CEOs and more. It's a great opportunity for social connection and to experience new ways of relating to one another.

FRIENDS

You can prototype hanging out with different circles of people to see which best suits your fancy. I've attended various events, festivals, and extracurriculars to see which people and groups resonate with me most. My main circles include alternative/hippie/Burning Man folks, entrepreneurs/geeks, and university friends. And sometimes I also roll with theatre friends I've met through improv or the musical productions I've written. Maybe your ideal crew is into grunge rock or swing dancing. You never know until you try it. The point here is that rather than automatically assuming the current things in your life are the best ones for you even if you haven't done much exploration, it could be good to expand your sphere of possibilities to see if there's something out there you haven't yet considered — a stone left unturned, that when revealed, could change your life.

Above are some of the ways you can prototype your life. What other areas of life do you think would be good to prototype or have you pro-totyped in the past? I'd love to hear about them. Feel free to send me an email through my website (jenniferturliuk.com). It might seem as if this suggestion of trying things out is something people already nat-urally do, but the prototyping process is a more disciplined and hope-fully more efficient way to go about things, in my opinion. It might also uncover something you haven't considered before, something that could change your life.

Closing Words

Be content with what you have, rejoice in the way
things are. When you realize nothing is lacking, the
whole world belongs to you.

— LAO TZU

FAILING UPWARD

I see my career like the graphic on the next page (a sine wave with increasing amplitude): a series of ups and downs that are bigger and bigger as you go along. This concept is similar to Cameron Herold's "The Emotional Rollercoaster of Entrepreneurs."[1]

Here are some samples from my life:

- I was very dissatisfied in a big corporation.
- After that, I started a self-education program involving Kiva and Airbnb.
- I lost an investment from Dave McClure because my co-founder abandoned me.
- But three days later I won financing from Start-Up Chile.

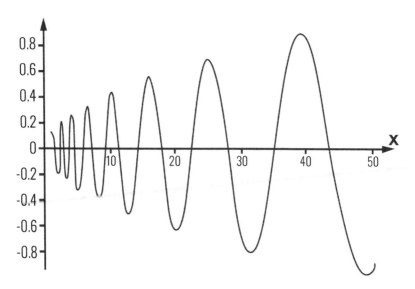

FIG. 18: *This sine wave with up-and-down amplitude can be applied to one's career path.* *Source: ©Matt Tweed. Used with permission.*

- My Start-Up Chile team split up.
- But one week later I won a scholarship to Singularity University.
- I had a bit of depression after the program.
- But later I was in the *New York Times*, *Fast Company*, and national television for my launch of a text message service tool to help victims of Hurricane Sandy.

You can see that in my view each failure comes with a success of equal magnitude. And if you want more success, you need to prepare yourself to have more failures, too. And the more you fail, the more you'll have success. Thanks to a job that was bad for me, I decided to leave and start this adventure of successes. Without that situation, it wouldn't be possible for me to be here today writing this book.

My recommendation is to view your career in a manner similar to the process of learning a new language. You need to try many things and take many risks and bad decisions to know what makes you happy and have great success.

I wish you the best of luck and would love it if you kept me updated with your progress along the way.

Appendix 1: Know Thyself Tools

ITEM	DONE?	LEARNING
Journal Writing		
Alone Time		
Digital Detox		
Substance Detox		
Meditation		
360-Degree Review		
Personality Tests		
Counsellors and Coaches		

ITEM	DONE?	LEARNING
Books, Articles, and Videos		
Balance		
To-Do List		
Know Thyself Questions		

FIG. 19: *Charting your to-do list.*

Appendix 2: Anonymous Reputation Survey[*]

_____'s **Anonymous Reputation Survey**

I really, really, really want you to be candid. Trust me — this is anonymous. Brevity is totally acceptable.

1. Gender? (Circle one.)
   (a) Male
   (b) Female
   (c) Prefer not to disclose

2. How do we (most) know each other? (Circle one.)
   (a) Work
   (b) School
   (c) Social
   (d) Other

3. In one to three words, how would you describe me?

_____

* Source: ©Kevin Rustagi. Used with permission.

4. What do I do well? (On my best day? As few words as you like.)

_____

_____

_____

5. What can I work on? (On my worst day? Again, feel free to say as little or as much as you like.)

_____

_____

_____

6. What is something about me that has stayed with you, good, bad, or otherwise? (Feel free to write one thing or multiple. Memories and stories, however brief, are super helpful. Again, this is totally anonymous.)

_____

_____

_____

7. Who am I interested in more? (Circle one.)

Myself   1   2   3   4   5   6   7   8   9   10   Others

8. Anything else about how you/others perceive me? (Optional.)

_____

_____

_____

THANK YOU for filling out my survey! ALL feedback is helpful. Regardless of what you wrote, I am so grateful.

Appendix 3: Know Thyself Questions

PART A: KNOW THYSELF

1. WHAT YOU LOVE

What did you love to do when you were a child?

_____

_____

_____

_____

_____

_____

_____

_____

What do you love to do?

_____

_____

_____

_____

_____

_____

What extracurriculars do you participate in/love?

_____

_____

_____

_____

_____

What are you doing when you feel the most alive? What are some activities that relax and rejuvenate you?

_____

_____

_____

_____

_____

_____

What topics do you love googling, reading about, learning about, or watching shows/films or listening to podcasts about?

_____

_____

_____

_____

_____

_____

What kinds of careers are the people you find yourself most interested in/attracted to doing?

_____

_____

_____

_____

_____

_____

What can you not stop thinking about?

_____

_____

_____

_____

_____

_____

What subjects did you love the most in school?

_____

_____

_____

_____

_____

_____

Who are some of the people you admire most and what do they do?

_____

_____

_____

_____

_____

_____

What did you like about your last job or your last few jobs? What didn't you like?

_____

_____

_____

_____

_____

What are some of your favourite places to be? Least favourite places?

_____

_____

_____

_____

_____

What are you most grateful for?

_____

_____

_____

_____

_____

What do you do without being paid, just because you love it? What would you do without being paid, because you love it that much?

_____

_____

_____

_____

_____

If you had 365 days left to live, what would you spend them doing?

_____

_____

_____

_____

_____

_____

What activities put you in such a state of flow that you lose track of time?

_____

_____

_____

_____

_____

What does your ideal day look like? (Days create a week, weeks create months, months create years, and years create a lifetime. But it all starts with a day, one cycle, so if you can get that cadence down, you can change your whole life. Change your days, change your life.)

_____

_____

_____

_____

_____

What kinds of people do you love to hang out with, or would you love to spend more time with? What are they like? What are the qualities of the types of people you'd most like to work with?

_____

_____

_____

_____

_____

_____

2. WHAT YOU CAN OFFER

What barriers or limitations do you have?

_____

_____

_____

_____

_____

Identify opposing/alternative thoughts to those barriers and limitations, or ways you can get around them in order to believe you have a chance of succeeding in finding a better career path for yourself.

_____

_____

_____

_____

_____

If you didn't feel these limitations, what would your life be like? What could you offer?

_____

_____

_____

_____

_____

_____

We each drag luggage around with us throughout life in the form of limitations and limiting beliefs. It's helpful to leave some baggage behind. Which of the above distorted thoughts about limitations would you like to leave behind?

_____

_____

_____

_____

_____

What's unique about you?

_____

_____

_____

_____

_____

What are some challenges you've faced and how could you parlay the strengths and knowledge you've developed as a result of helping others, e.g. those with similar challenges?

_____

_____

_____

_____

_____

_____

What are your strengths?

_____

_____

_____

_____

_____

_____

What do your friends/peers/colleagues routinely come to you for advice on? (Leave space for people to answer these questions.)

_____

_____

_____

_____

_____

_____

What subjects were you best at in school?

_____

_____

_____

_____

_____

3. WHAT YOU NEED

What are your values? (Rank them from 1 to 5. Examples: health, family, et cetera.)

_____

_____

_____

_____

_____

_____

To you, what is work? What's the meaning of work? What sort of value does it have? (These are questions Steve Jobs was rumoured to have asked a Buddhism teacher when he was young.)

_____

_____

_____

_____

_____

How much money do you want and/or need to make over the course of your career? By when? What sort of annual salary do you want to command now and in the future? What will you do with that money (e.g. what will you buy)? (As part of your decision, understand that after an income level of $75,000, increases in salary haven't been shown to make a material impact on happiness. As well, intrinsic goals (personal growth, feeling of community, inherent satisfaction) are much more fulfilling than extrinsic goals (money, image, status, popularity).

_____

_____

_____

_____

_____

_____

_____

_____

_____

_____

4. HOW YOU WANT TO HELP THE WORLD

How do you wish the world could be different? What kind of culture do you want to live in?

_____

_____

_____

_____

What kind of legacy do you want to leave?

_____

_____

_____

_____

Another way you can get to the root of things is by identifying a series of "why's," e.g. if you wrote "I want to change education," you could write a follow-up question of "Why?" and answer it. Doing this five of six times will help you get past initial thoughts and go deeper, figuring out what the true essence is behind what you want to do. So, go for it. Write a few statements of how you want the world to be different or what kind of legacy you want to leave, then write five why's and answers for each.

_____

_____

_____

_____

_____

_____

What's the purpose of your life?

_____

_____

_____

_____

_____

5.   CHARACTERISTICS OF YOUR IDEAL NEXT STEP

What are you looking for in a next opportunity? (Keep in mind that we're not really considering specific titles or companies right now, just broad categories. That will come later.)

Salary: _____

Hours: _____

Time Off: _____

Location: _____

Size of Company: _____

Culture: _____

PART B: KNOW YOUR OPTIONS

What careers might potentially be a fit for you? What might you like to do?

_____

_____

_____

_____

_____

Trends:

_____

_____

_____

_____

List of Careers You Could Invent:

_____

_____

_____

_____

_____

_____

1. CUTTING DOWN YOUR LIST

What are your hard limits or no-go zones? (For example: "I don't want to work for a company that promotes smoking.")

_____

_____

_____

_____

_____

_____

What might make a job not feasible, possible, or interesting for you? (For example: "I don't really know if I want to move.")

_____

_____

_____

_____

Use the above questions to cut down your career list. The table below shows you how to do this. Plot the careers across the X axis and the criteria along the Y axis. Next, assess each career's fit with each criterion, i.e., yes or no. From here, you should be able to eliminate some options.

	Doctor	Dietician	Physiotherapist
Cannot make under $40,000 annually	Yes	Yes	Yes
Don't want to move	No	Yes	Yes

Now it's your turn:

Your Turn			

You should now be left with a list of career options that could be possible for you. You'll have crossed out ones that aren't possible because of facts and noted which ones might not be possible based on what you find out about whether the assumptions you had were right or wrong (in a next step). In my example above, I crossed out doctor and had dietician and physiotherapist remaining. Write out the options here. Recall that these categories can and should be broad, e.g. "something in hospitals." This will be a first cut, and as I said, more will be cut later. We'll also get to specific job titles later.

List of careers that could be possible:

_____

_____

_____

_____

_____

_____

_____

List of careers that could be possible if assumptions turn out okay:

_____

_____

_____

_____

_____

_____

_____

2. YOUR IDEAL WORK ENVIRONMENT

Place yourself on a scale somewhere on one end of these diametric opposites. For example:

Small Company  Big Company

I placed myself closer to "small company" because I want to be part of a small company. But not too small!

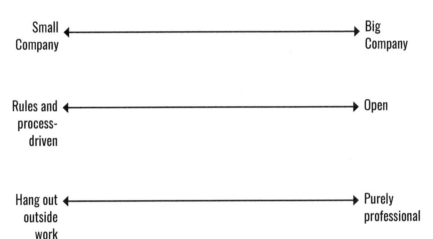

Small Company ←————————————→ Big Company

Rules and process-driven ←————————————→ Open

Hang out outside work ←————————————→ Purely professional

Looking at the career options through this lens will help you narrow your list further.

My list of potential career options now:

_____

_____

_____

_____

_____

3. ONE MORE CHECK

Make sure, if you haven't already, to:

- Cross out careers that you:
  - Can't do (practical limitations).
  - Won't do (e.g. morally against, don't want to move, et cetera).
- Identify careers that you:
  - Might not be able to do (assumptions).
- Cross-reference know-thyself results:
  - Narrow options based on that (e.g. hours, pay).

Your list of potential career options:

_____

_____

_____

_____

_____

4. IDENTIFY OPTIONS

In this step, you'll want to identify your options from your last round of narrowing. Since you're starting this cycle for the first time, your options will be left over from step 3. In the chart below, you can see how I identified my remaining options on the right, including the career I had an assumption about: venture capital.

What Careers Might Potentially Be a Fit (What I Might Like Doing)?	Options
• Join a startup.	• Join a startup.
• Start a startup.	• Start a startup.
• Work at a non-profit.	• Work at a non-profit.
• Start a non-profit.	• Start a non-profit.
• Venture capital.	• Venture capital.
· Assumption: that I could get a job in VC.	· Assumption: that I could get a job in VC.
• International development work.	
· Too far from family.	

My options:

_____

_____

_____

_____

_____

5. IDENTIFY MVCs

Note how the commitment deepens at each step:

My Chosen MVCs

A. Read online articles about logistics of jobs (30 min. each).

B. Watch talks about jobs (1 hr. each).

C. Informational interviews (2 hrs. each).

D. Shadowing (1 day).

E. Shadowing (5 days).

Acknowledgements

Thank you to Scott Fraser, publisher and president of Dundurn Press, for believing in this project. Big thanks to my agent, Robert Mackwood of Seventh Avenue Literary Agency, for the amazing support and encouragement; and to my editor, Michael Carroll, for your sage guidance through my first book-editing process. Thanks to my publicist, Heather Wood, for getting the word out about my book. Thank you to managing editor Elena Radic for being so awesome and on top of things the whole way through, and to art director and designer Laura Boyle for the awesome cover! Thank you to editorial assistant and proofreader Melissa Kawaguchi for finding ways to make this book better. Thanks also to the rest of the incredible team at Dundurn: Kathryn Lane, Jenny McWha, Rudi Garcia, Sophie Paas-Lang, Kendra Martin, Lisa Marie Smith, Ankit Pahwa, Sara D'Agostino, Kayleigh Fisher, and Sylvie Xiao.

Thank you to *Muse* and *Forbes* for the opportunity to write about my journey, and to all the readers who shared their stories and encouraged me to write this book. Thanks, too, to early readers of this book for your feedback and inspiration.

Big shout-out to the smiling staff at the coffee shop where I wrote most of this book, and to Lisa and my incredible writing community whom I wrote alongside for providing a positive atmosphere of accountability and encouragement.

Thank you to Queen's University and Singularity University, without which I wouldn't be where I am today. To my colleagues, thank you for inspiring me every day.

I'm grateful for my friends, who add such joy to life — you know who you are.

Thanks so much to my family for always being there for me — to Mum, Dad, Steve, Nana, and Maya. Mum, thank you for being the original promoter of this book and for giving early drafts to your friends! Their feedback was invaluable, and readers wouldn't be holding this book today without it.

And thanks of course to my canine companion Lexi — though she may not be able to read this, I am sending her my love.

And, of course, thank you to those who let me shadow them, those whom I met with, the great education programs I attended, the wonderful people I encountered, those who gave great talks, those who wrote amazing books, and to all the places that I lived.

Notes

Introduction

1. Sharecare, "Community Well-Being Index: The World's Most Definitive Measurement of Well-Being" (2019), wellbeingindex .sharecare.com; Marc Montgomery, "Only About One-Quarter of Canadians Satisfied with Their Job," Radio Canada International, December 17, 2018, rcinet.ca/en/2018/12/17 /only-about-one-quarter-of-canadians-satisfied-with-their-job.
2. Jennifer Turliuk, "How I Figured Out What I Wanted to Do with My Life," *Forbes*, June 27, 2012, forbes.com/sites/ dailymuse/2012/06/27/how-i-figured-out-what-i-wanted-to-do -with-my-life/#4a476d513883.

Chapter 1: The Career Crisis

1. Sharecare, "Community Well-Being Index"; Montgomery, "Only About One-Quarter of Canadians Satisfied with Their Job."

2. Deloitte, "The Paradox of Flows: Can Hope Flow from Fear?," 2016 Shift Index, deloitte.com/us/en/pages/center-for-the-edge/topics/deloitte-shift-index-series.html.

3. Mercer, "Inside Employees' Minds: The Transforming Employment Experience," September 2015, mercer.com.hk/content/dam/mercer/attachments/global/inside-employees-minds/inside-employees-minds-united-states-report-part-one.pdf; John Hollon, "Survey: Half of Employees Want to Leave or Have Checked Out on the Job," Talent Management & HR, June 21, 2011, tlnt.com/survey-half-of-employees-want-to-leave-or-have-checked-out-on-the-job.

4. NORC at the University of Chicago, "The General Social Survey," (2016), gss.norc.org/About-The-GSS.

5. Lydia Saad, "In U.S., Worries About Job Cutbacks Return to Record Highs," Gallup, August 31, 2011, news.gallup.com/poll/149261/worries-job-cutbacks-return-record-highs.aspx.

6. Michael Argyle, "Do Happy Workers Work Harder? The Effect of Job Satisfaction on Work Performance," in *How Harmful Is Happiness: Consequences of Enjoying Life or Not*, ed. Ruut Veenhoven (Rotterdam: Universitaire Pers Rotterdam, 1989), www2.eur.nl/fsw/research/veenhoven/Pub1980s/89a-C9-full.pdf.

7. Randy Komisar and Kent Lineback, *The Monk and the Riddle: The Education of a Silicon Valley Entrepreneur* (Boston: Harvard Business School Press, 2000), 154.

8. Susan Sorenson and Keri Garman, "How to Tackle U.S. Employees' Stagnating Engagement," Gallup, June 11 2013, news.gallup.com/businessjournal/162953/tackle-employees-stagnating-engagement.aspx.

9. Larry Stybel, "Murray's Law for Success on Your Own Terms," *Harvard Business Review*, July 21, 2011, hbr.org/2011/07/murrays-law-for-success-on-you.

10. Elena Andreeva et al., "Depressive Symptoms as a Cause and Effect of Job Loss in Men and Women: Evidence in the Context of Organisational Downsizing from the Swedish Longitudinal Occupational Survey of Health," *BMC Public Health* 15, no. 1045 (October 12, 2015); ncbi.nlm.nih.gov/pmc/articles/PMC4603822; Argyle, "Do Happy Workers Work Harder?"

Chapter 2: Life and Career as a Series of Tests

1. John Krumboltz, "Practical Career Counseling Applications of the Happenstance Learning Theory," in *APA Handbook of Career Intervention, Vol. 2: Applications*, eds. P.J. Hartung et al. (Washington, DC: American Psychological Association, 2015), 283–92, psycnet .apa.org/doiLanding?doi=10.1037%2F14439-021.
2. Eric Ries, *The Lean Startup: How Today's Entrepreneurs Use Continuous Innovation to Create Radically Successful Businesses* (New York: Crown, 2011).

Chapter 3: Introducing the Prototyping Your Career Method

1. Steve Blank, *The Four Steps to the Epiphany: Successful Strategies for Products That Win* (Hoboken, NJ: John Wiley & Sons, 2020); Ries, *The Lean Startup*.

Chapter 4: Step 1: Understanding Current Research

1. Lapels Dry Cleaning, "Dry Cleaning Franchises Produce More Millionaires Than Any Other Franchise — Fact or Fiction?," Franchising.com, franchising.com/news/20130930_dry_cleaning_franchises_produce_more_millionaires_.html.
2. Komisar and Lineback, *The Monk and the Riddle*.
3. Reid Hoffman and Ben Casnocha, *The Start-Up of You: Adapt to the Future, Invest in Yourself, and Transform Your Career* (New York: Currency, 2012).
4. Ryan Holiday, *The Obstacle Is the Way: The Timeless Art of Turning Trials into Triumph* (New York: Penguin, 2014).
5. Bruce Feiler, *Life Is in the Transitions: Mastering Change at Any Age* (New York: Penguin, 2020).
6. Tom Rath, *Strengths Finder 2.0* (New York: Gallup Press, 2007).

7. Belinda Luscombe, "Do We Need $75,000 to Be Happy?," *Time*, September 6, 2010, content.time.com/times/magazine/article/0,9171,2019628,00.html.

8. Richard Bach, *Jonathan Livingstone Seagull* (New York: Scribner, 2014).

Chapter 5: Step 2: Casting a Net

1. Stacy E. Walker, "Journal Writing as a Teaching Technique to Promote Reflection," *Journal of Athletic Training* 41, no. 2 (2006): 216–21, ncbi.nlm.nih.gov/pmc/articles/PMC1472640; Lisa Tams, "Journaling to Reduce Stress," Michigan State University, May 1, 2013, canr.msu.edu/news/journaling_to_reduce_stress.

2. Julia Cameron, *The Artist's Way: A Spiritual Path to Higher Creativity* (New York: Tarcher, 2016).

3. Paul Graham, "How to Do What You Love," Gallup, January 2006, paulgraham.com/love.html?viewfullsite=1.

4. *The Five-Minute Journal* (Toronto: Intelligent Change, 2015).

5. Charlotte vanOyen-Witvliet et al., "Gratitude Predicts Hope and Happiness: A Two-Study Assessment of Traits and States," *The Journal of Positive Psychology* 14, no. 3 (2019): 271–82, digital-commons.hope.edu/cgi/viewcontent.cgi?article=2591&context =faculty_publications.

6. Leo Babauta, *Essential Zen Habits: Mastering the Art of Change, Briefly* (Pipe Dreams Publishing, 2015).

7. Igor Pantic, "Online Social Networking and Mental Health," *Cyberpsychology, Behaviour and Social Networking* 17, no. 10 (October 1, 2014): 652–57, ncbi.nlm.nih.gov/pmc/articles /PMC4183915; Melissa G. Hunt et al., "No More FOMO: Limiting Social Media Decreases Loneliness and Depression," *Journal of Social & Clinical Psychology* 37, no. 10 (2018): 751–68, guilfordjournals.com/doi/10.1521/jscp.2018.37.10.751.

8. Daniel Campos et al., "Meditation and Happiness: Mindfulness and Self-Compassion May Mediate the Meditation-Happiness Relationship," *Personality and Individual Differences* 93 (September

2015), researchgate.net/publication/281643912_Meditation_and_happiness_Mindfulness_and_self-compassion_may_mediate_the_meditation-happiness_relationship.

9. World Health Organization, "Mental Disorders Affect One in Four People" (2001), who.int/whr/2001/media_centre/press_release/en/#:~:text=Geneva%2C%204%20October%E2%80%94%20One%20in,ill%2Dhealth%20and%20disability%20worldwide.

10. Richard N. Bolles, *What Color Is Your Parachute?* (New York: Ten Speed Press, 2019).

11. Tim Clark, Alexander Osterwalder, and Yves Pigneur, *Business Model You: A One-Page Method for Reinventing Your Career* (Hoboken, NJ: John Wiley & Sons, 2012).

12. Hoffman and Casnocha, *The Start-Up of You.*

13. Clayton M. Christensen, James Allworth, and Karen Dillon, *How Will You Measure Your Life?* (New York: HarperCollins, 2012).

14. TED Talks, "Talks to Help You Find the Right Job," ted.com/playlists /220/7_talks_to_help_you_find_the_r; Daphne Blake, "The 10 Best TED Talks to Watch for Choosing a Career," Hubworks, hubworks .com/blog/the-ten-best-ted-talks-to-watch-for-choosing-a-career .html; Workopolis, "Top 10 Motivational TED Talks for Your Career," careers.workopolis.com/advice/top-10-motivational-ted-talks-career.

Chapter 9: Step 4.2: Minimum Viable Commitments (MVCs)

1. Timothy Ferriss, *The 4-Hour Workweek: Escape the 9–5, Live Anywhere and Join the New Rich* (New York: Harmony, 2009).

Chapter 14: Your Top Three

1. Paul Graham, "The Top Idea in Your Mind," July 2010, paulgraham .com/top.html.

Chapter 15: Closing the Deal

1. Marianne Williamson, *A Return to Love: Reflections on the Principles of "A Course in Miracles"* (New York: HarperCollins, 1992).

Chapter 16: Land the Job

1. Carol S. Dweck, *Mindset: How You Can Fulfil Your Potential* (London: Constable & Robinson, 2012).

Chapter 20: Interviewing

1. "Form 990 of Toastmasters International Inc. for Fiscal Year 2016," Department of the Treasury, Internal Revenue Service, apps.irs.gov/pub/epostcard/cor/951300076_201612_990_2018010915102275.pdf.

Chapter 21: Make Your Own Job

1. Verne Harnish, *Scaling Up: How a Few Companies Make It … and Why the Rest Don't* (Ashburn, VA: Gazelles, 2014).
2. Geoff Smart and Randy Street, *Who: The A Method for Hiring* (New York: Ballantine, 2008).
3. Bradford D. Smart, *Topgrading: The Proven Hiring and Promoting Method That Turbocharges Company Performance* (New York: Penguin, 2012).

Chapter 23: For Students

1. Thad Peterson, "How Good Is Education at Predicting Job Performance?," The Predictive Index, October 3, 2017,

predictiveindex.com/blog/how-good-is-education-at-predicting
-job-performance.

Chapter 24: Make Your Own Blueprint

1. Anthony K. Tjan, "Entrepreneurial DNA: Do You Have It?," Harvard
    Business Review, April 29, 2009, hbr.org/2009/04/entrepreneurial
    -dna-do-you-hav.

Chapter 25: Prototyping Life

1. Franklin Veaux and Eve Rickert, *More Than Two: A Practical Guide
    to Ethical Polyamory* (Portland, OR: Thorntree Press, 2014).
2. Tim Ferriss, *The 4-Hour Body* (New York: Crown Archetype, 2010).

Closing Words

1. Cameron Herold, "The Emotional Rollercoaster of Entrepreneurs,"
    in Tim Ferriss, "Harnessing Entrepreneurial Manic-Depression:
    Making the Rollercoaster Work for You," *Tim Ferriss* (blog) October
    3, 2008, tim.blog/2008/10/03/harnessing-entrepreneurial-manic
    -depression-making-the-rollercoaster-work-for-you.

Index

Page numbers in italics refer to figures or appendices.

About the Author

Jennifer Turliuk is an entrepreneur, writer, and speaker. Her work has been featured in the *New York Times*, *Huffington Post*, *Fast Company*, *Wired*, and more. She attended Queen's University and Singularity University (at NASA) and was awarded an honorary degree from Humber College for her contributions to society. Jennifer's writing can be found in *Forbes*, *Business Insider*, *Strategy*, and various newspapers.